PRAISE FOR UNSHAKEA~~BLE INFLUENCE~~

"Daniel shares a practical and powerful argument: our power and influence arise from not just our own excellent work, but from our absolutely essential inner game that steers our actions. He reminds us that our authentic and powerful leadership derives from our inner bearings and stability, not from our corner office. His guidance on cultivating that winning inner game should be required reading for all C-Suites."

- Michael Carboy, Former Executive Vice President, OC Oerlikon

"In UNSHAKEABLE INFLUENCE, Daniel Kimble quickly grabs attention with adrenaline-filled racing stories then hands us the keys to build our own best and authentic leadership. By learning to manage ourselves with introspection and self-honesty, and build trust while racing wheel-to-wheel at 100 miles per hour."

- Patrick Lough, Vice President, First American

"I raced through UNSHAKEABLE INFLUENCE – it's a real thrill to learn from a framework that shows me both how to be a better leader and a better person. Unshakeable Influence is packed with insightful truths about the human condition and practical suggestions for how to improve our leadership capabilities."

- John Grover, Chief People Officer, Endsight

"UNSHAKEABLE INFLUENCE does what no other business book out there does: it helps leaders master their rarely spoken about "inner game" to enhance their ability to influence. Finally! A practical resource that teaches us how to take what all of us have inside – our thoughts and feelings – and maximize them to be effective 21st century leaders."

- Katherine McGrady, PhD, President and CEO, CNA

"UNSHAKEABLE INFLUENCE is captivating through illustrations on how each of our actions and behaviors influence our leadership capabilities – and, in turn, our resulting personal and organizational successes or failures. Daniel provides convincing and entertaining examples demonstrating ways in which we can improve results and satisfaction by balancing our mind, heart, and soul."

UNSHAKEABLE INFLUENCE

Mastering the Inner Game of Leadership

in a VUCA World

Dear Maggie,
    I hope you enjoy
my book.
                Warmly,
                Daniel Kimble

DANIEL KIMBLE

UNSHAKEABLE INFLUENCE:
Mastering the Inner Game of Leadership in a VUCA World

Disclaimer: This book is designed to provide accurate and authoritative information in regard to the subject matter covered. By its sale, neither the publisher nor the author is engaged in rendering psychological or other professional services. If expert assistance is needed, the services of a competent professional should be sought.

For Indy

"Knowing others is intelligence; knowing yourself is true wisdom. Mastering others is strength; mastering yourself is true power. If you realize that you have enough, you are truly rich." Lao Tzu

Contents

Foreword

AS I'M WRITING THIS in December of 2020, it has been 20 months since the first edition of Unshakeable Influence was published. In that time, two key things have occurred that led me to conclude that a second edition was warranted.

First, over these 20 months I have developed a more thorough understanding of my own material by observing and learning from the way in which the book has been received by business leaders. Second, what we have experienced in 2020 has made everyone painfully aware of just how VUCA (Volatile, Uncertain, Complex, Ambiguous) the world can be.

When I was writing the first edition of Unshakeable Influence in 2018-19, I cannot claim to have foreseen everything that 2020 had in store for us. But I did foresee the urgent need for leaders to focus more on their Inner Game of Leadership as this is the most effective way to lead with all the complexities, uncertainties, ambiguities, and volatilities of the modern business world.

As such, this second edition of Unshakeable Influence is written and edited to clearly illustrate the importance of mastering our Inner Game of Leadership so that we can not only increase our tolerance for VUCA, but learn to truly thrive as leaders in today's VUCA world.

DANIEL KIMBLE

Acknowledgments

WITHOUT THE GENEROUS SUPPORT of a loving family, friends, colleagues, and editors, this book simply would not exist. Or perhaps a lesser version of this book would have made the world yawn and then immediately sunk into oblivion. Whatever level of impact this book might ultimately have, I owe a lot of that to others.

First and foremost, my parents deserve acknowledgment. On top of the fact that this book would not exist if they had not created me, they've been there for me in so many ways over the years that I can't even count. My dad is one of my best friends. And my mom has always shown undying support for her children to a degree that few mothers do.

As a child of nine years old, I had begun to write a book about how and why adults don't understand their children. Ironically, I soon destroyed that book in anger after an argument with my dad. As I drew close to completing this book, I realized that in some unexpected way this book is a continuation of that writing journey I embarked on as a boy.

My adult journey toward writing this book certainly began in a leadership communications class in UC Berkeley's Executive MBA program in November 2010. Dr. Mark Rittenberg opened me up to who I am. He is a great coach who not only gave me a glimpse of what I have in me but led me through a set of experiences that exposed the deepest parts of me that had been dormant for so long.

Standing on a chair singing a full-hearted (yet completely out of tune) happy birthday to my son Indy, who turned one year old the week of that course, is a moment I will never forget. Later that same day, reading Walt Whitman's poem O Me! O Life! while I led the class through a re-enactment of the closing scene from the movie *Dead Poets Society* – moving Professor Rittenberg to tears – was also a priceless awakening experience.

The next big highlight on my journey leading up to this book came through my experiences training with the Coaches Training Institute (CTI). A number of faculty members there have been significant in my life, most of all Susan Carlisle for her brilliant coaching of me for a number of years. And an acknowledgement of CTI would not be complete if I didn't give a shout out to Sam House and Carey Baker. My experiences assisting them in leading a leadership program were invaluable. They welcomed me, invited me in, and - whether they knew it at the time or not - served as key teachers at that point in my life. Thank you both.

Next up in the long list of people who have contributed to this book are Angelique Rewers and Phil Dyer. They were the first to see in me the ability to grow into a thought leader in the field of leadership development. I couldn't believe it myself when they first put that to me, but I've relentlessly focused on growing into that ever since. This book would not exist if it wasn't for their catalyzing effect on me. I also want to thank David Neagle, another key mentor of mine. And I'm eternally grateful to Brynne Dippell for her spiritual guidance and healing.

I also want to thank each and every one of my company's past, present, and future clients. I learn from you just like you learn from me. Thanks for your belief in me and my organization, your willingness to play and experiment, and your hunger for more. You are a constant fuel for me in my relentless pursuit of all of us becoming our best selves. This book would not be possible if not for all of my experiences with you, and I can't wait for what's next!

I'm also standing on the shoulders of so many amazing friends, colleagues, coaches, teachers, thought leaders, researchers, authors, and speakers who all have had a formative effect on this book. There are far too many to name... Thanks to you all!

My wife Marianne has been wonderful in her support of my obsession with getting this book done in such a way that I can be forever proud. Thank you for your constant support and for giving an amazing level of editing advice that only a fellow author could possibly offer. Thank you for your deep understanding, support, and wisdom. You, your love, your beauty - and the relationship we're creating together - constantly inspire me!

Finally, I want to thank my son Indiana, to whom this book is dedicated. Indy, there is no one who inspires me more than you. You show a level of love, compassion, and wisdom that astounds me coming from anyone, let alone a young boy. I will always love you like a billion, zillion, quintillion circles, big man!

Introduction

AS MY BODY TUMBLED across the pavement at 100 miles per hour (mph) like a rag doll, all I could see was a coiling blur of ground, sky, ground sky, ground sky. As crazy as it sounds, the only thought going through my mind in those few, grueling moments was, *I hope I can still make my race on Sunday.*

I imagine you can relate to the desire to be the best at something. To really excel. To be number one. That was my goal that racing season. I was laser-focused on winning the championship in my motorcycle racing class. At the time of my crash, I was leading the points race in my class, and only half a season remained.

I was on track to win it all.

Yet there I was, two days before the next race, tumbling across the pavement at 100 mph.

Ground, sky, ground, sky, ground, sky.

I wasn't thinking about my health. I wasn't thinking about how slamming across the pavement like a human cannonball could seriously injure or even kill me.

The only thing I was thinking about was getting the result.

I wanted to win.

Eventually, I stopped tumbling. In the few minutes it took to get my bearings and shake off the physical trauma of the crash, I honestly didn't know if I was all right. When I finally managed to sit up, I breathed a deep sigh of relief. I was okay. Nothing broken. No gaping wounds.

I looked for my motorcycle and saw it had come to a stop about 200 feet away from where I'd landed. Even from that distance, I could tell that it was totaled and would need a lot of work to get it ready for my race on Sunday, only two short days away.

I spent the rest of that day down in the pits surrounded by tarmac in 100-degree heat rebuilding my bike. The spare parts I'd brought with me for that race were helpful, but I quickly discovered that I didn't have everything I needed to get the job done. Luckily, some of my competitors were kind enough to lend me the parts I was missing, so I could build a new bike from scratch.

At the end of the day, I had a bike that was in working order. Or so I thought. Taking it for a test ride, I realized it wasn't handling right at all, and I soon figured out that the frame (pretty much the only thing I hadn't replaced) was bent. Upon inspection during the rebuild, I hadn't caught this problem. It's not possible to ride safely with a bent frame, let alone race at top speeds, so I spent the entire next day rebuilding the bike all over again with another frame.

Thankfully, I made the race the next day, but I'll admit I was not at my best. Crashing at 100 mph messes with your mind. I noticed I felt hesitant on the bike, a feeling I wasn't used to. I was also physically fatigued from the impact tumbling across pavement had on my body, along with two full days spent in 100-degree heat rebuilding my bike not just once, but twice.

I placed fourth in the race that day, which was pretty good all things considered, but I'd needed to place first or second to maintain the points lead in my class and keep the momentum I'd been creating that season. I fell out of the points lead, and my main rival took over that slot.

I never recovered from falling behind. My rival ended up winning it all, and that changed my perspective on leadership and life forever.

Just like my big crash woke me up, so too is this book a wake-up call to business leaders. As we've seen in 2020, the outside world can be fickle. It's never been more important to learn how to be a great leader in a VUCA world. For decades, business leaders have been too focused on the external impact their position affords them – how positional authority affects others in their race to have it all. Fame. Fortune. Turnarounds. Buyouts. Acquisitions. Mergers. Yet each of these outcomes is directly correlated to how much the strongest leadership currency of all - *influence* - is in play.

In the race for leaders to adapt to our VUCA world, mastering the Inner Game of Leadership is the primary factor. Without a great Inner Game of Leadership our very core as leaders is unstable. As a result, everything we create from that place is also unstable. When we have cultivated a rock-solid inner game as leaders, we become unshakeable in our influence and then the outer game of leadership flows quite easily. Unshakeable influence in a VUCA world, therefore, requires mastering the *Inner* Game of Leadership much more than the *outer* game everyone sees.

In my 1:1 work with some of the world's most powerful business leaders, I've seen firsthand how Mastering their Inner Game of Leadership causes them to become more powerful, more resilient, and more effective leaders. That's because the Inner Game of Leadership is purpose-driven, relationship-focused, and based on the strongest leadership currency of all—influence. By becoming unshakeable in their influence, these leaders consistently get the most out of everyone in their organization through *who they're being* - as leaders and as human beings.

This book aims to answer crucial questions about mastering the Inner Game of Leadership and what it takes to develop unshakeable influence in a VUCA world, including:

- How does mastering our Inner Game of Leadership enable us to thrive in a VUCA world?
- What are the thoughts, feelings, behaviors, and strategies that help us exert influence over ourselves and others?
- How can we excel at creating and directing our thoughts, feelings, and behaviors so they are in alignment with where we want to go and best support us and our organizations in the pursuit of excellence?

- How do we create a safe 'internal' environment where we honor our hearts, minds, and souls so that the external environment flows optimally?
- How do we get stuff done, achieve great results, and inspire people to be their best without sacrificing one for another?
- What does excellence look like, and what does it mean?

I read lots of leadership books and many of them present solid theories about what it is to be a great leader. These books often offer tools, tips, exercises, and the like. All of this can be helpful. But unlike what is available in the marketplace, this book zooms in on what I believe is the most important element of great leadership: the Inner Game of Leadership.

All of us, whether we know it or not, care at some level about our leadership and life legacy. Yet many of us rarely know how to be our best selves day in and day out in service to bringing about our best legacy. While we may be leading and living in a good enough way that has garnered us some success, failing to master the Inner Game of Leadership is costly. Without it, we might live a comfortable life, perhaps even a very nice life. But are we leading an inspired life? Are we living up to our fullest potential? Are we ready for the unforeseen, and yet inevitable, disruptions ahead of us? Are we creating the kind of life we will feel completely proud of at the end? In my view, the only way we can create and sustain the optimal results we want for ourselves, our organizations, and the world, is to master and fine-tune our Inner Game of Leadership.

I've experienced leadership in a lot of different arenas: the motorcycle racing world, the corporate world of Silicon Valley, and for years now as an executive coach and leader of leaders. Further, as I'm writing this second edition in the midst of the COVID-19 pandemic of 2020, I'm being called to step up in an even bigger way. Like so many businesses this year, we experienced a shock and a lot of uncertainty in the first part of 2020 when the pandemic took hold here in the United States.

This disruption challenged me to draw even deeper from the well of my internal resources with everything I've got, putting into sharp relief my own limits alongside the actions I had to take if I wanted myself and my business to thrive in this new reality. It's certainly been an interesting and challenging twist on my leadership adventure. Like rebuilding a motorcycle after a crash, I had to use parts already on hand, build new parts to make some wholesale improvements, and thereby put myself and my organization together in a new, more powerful, and more resilient way. And now as I write this in December of 2020, I look back on the year with pride and knowledge that we managed to create our best year yet, in spite of some difficult and unexpected challenges. My own Inner Game of Leadership journey will never be over, but it is always a thrilling ride. And while there are inevitable setbacks, when using the tools in this book, the overall trend is a never-ending upward spiral.

At the end of the day, we cannot anticipate all the obstacles and pitfalls that may show up during our race. What we can do is maximize our ability to recover and quickly adapt in this VUCA world. It all starts with how you choose to relate to the material in this book. I encourage you to take the time to go beyond simply consuming the ideas in this book and devote time to answering the questions and doing the exercises that complement the information. Most of all, you need to take what's in this book and apply it in your day-to-day leadership if you want to become unshakeable in your influence and become a great leader. For anyone who has more questions about how to do this, please see the "About the Author" section at the end of the book for ways to connect with me and my organization.

In deciding how to conceptualize and organize this book, I created a model to represent the key elements of mastering our Inner Game of Leadership. See figure I.1.

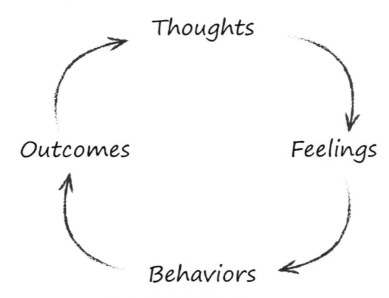

Figure I.1 – Thoughts->Feelings->Behaviors->Outcomes Model

As the model illustrates, thoughts create feelings; feelings create behaviors; and behaviors create outcomes. Those outcomes then feed our thoughts, and the cycle begins anew.

One of my business school professors liked to say, "All models are wrong. Some are useful." Like any useful model, this one is a simplification. First, in reality it's not as linear as the model suggests. Second, the actual feedback loop is not just one directional, but multi-directional. Third, while there is a predominant flow from thoughts to feelings to behaviors to outcomes, in actuality all facets on this model also directly influence all other facets. However, to work toward mastering each of these components within ourselves, it is useful to distill the complex topic of the Inner Game of Leadership down to this model and then use this model as a guide for structuring the book.

Thus, I've organized this book into four parts and a conclusion:

Part 1: Gearing Up for the Leadership Race of the 21st Century
Part 2: Mindset *(thoughts)*
Part 3: Heartset *(feelings)*

Part 4: Putting It into Practice *(behaviors)*
Conclusion *(outcomes)*

Within each part, I explore how that particular theme plays a role in mastering our Inner Game of Leadership so we can develop unshakeable influence. Part 1 helps you prepare to get the most out of this book. Part 2 introduces Mindset (our established set of beliefs and attitudes and the habitual thoughts that we have about ourselves and the world) and details the Mindset skills needed to master our Inner Game of Leadership. Part 3 introduces Heartset (our prevailing emotional tone, our ability to constructively navigate the emotions of ourselves and others, and our habitual ways of interacting and communicating with others) and details the Heartset skills needed to master our Inner Game of Leadership. Part 4 highlights how to apply our improved Mindset and Heartset skills in tangible, real-world situations that many executives face. And finally, the conclusion ties it all together and summarizes what is next for us once we've sufficiently mastered our Inner Game of Leadership. Like a well-tuned motorcycle, all the parts presented in this book are designed to work together if we are to have any hope of competing in the leadership race of the 21st century.

In today's fast-paced, ever-changing, and hyper-connected world, our title and our position on the organizational chart matter less than ever before. True leadership power comes down to how well we can influence others by carrying ourselves in a way that inspires, motivates, and brings out the best in people. A move from the positional to the relational is paramount. This requires a fundamental shift in Mindset and Heartset from positional authority to relational authority.

While leaders everywhere are facing more challenges than ever before in today's VUCA world, I believe we are living in one of the most exciting times of human history. This is a time of unprecedented change, turmoil, and uncertainty. And with such massive change, turmoil, and uncertainty comes an opportunity for wholesale improvements across the board. But to do that, we've got to learn how to be a great leader during VUCA circumstances. Mastering the Inner Game of Leadership has never been more important. If we choose to accept the call of this book, unshakeable influence will be within our reach.

In the following pages, I explore and examine what mastering the Inner Game of Leadership is, what it looks like, and what it ultimately means for individuals and the organizations they work for. Everyone is a leader. Whether someone is sitting in the C-Suite at a multi-billion-dollar global conglomerate, a mid-level leader at a smaller organization, an individual contributor, an entrepreneur, a house-spouse, or even a child, everyone is a leader. Regardless of the roles we play in life, every minute of every day, we can choose to either show up as a leader or not. This book is about relating to ourselves in new and more powerful ways by showing how to maximize our Mindset and Heartset so that we not only lead in a more resilient and impactful way, but learn to thrive under any circumstance so that we are well prepared for today's VUCA world.

This book explores how the Inner Game of Leadership works and why it is the most important factor in unmasking our deepest leadership power. The book also provides practical tips for recognizing, responding to, and optimizing what is going on inside us. What emotions and thoughts are we having in the present moment? How are these thoughts and emotions serving us and driving us toward our goals or causing us to crash and burn at 100 mph?

Mastering your Inner Game of Leadership is not an easy path, but if you persist, I'm sure you will be pleasantly surprised at how much this inner work pays off over time. While reading this book, I ask that you do your best to suspend any disbelief you may have long enough to complete the book and put some of this into practice. To those who stay the course, the transformation to becoming unshakeable in your influence is palpable and powerful. I've seen this transformation happen again and again with my clients, and this book makes that transformation available to you, too.

PART 1

Gearing Up for the Leadership Race of the 21st Century

Chapter 1

The Business Case for Mastering Your Inner Game of Leadership

I'VE HAD THE PRIVILEGE of working in Silicon Valley for more than thirty-five years. My experiences range from production-line worker at a semiconductor fabrication company at the age of 17 to a global program manager reporting to a COO for a multi-billion-dollar technology organization. I've worked for some of the biggest name companies in the technology industry, and I've founded two successful companies of my own. I've also had the privilege of graduating from two of the best business schools in the world. In all my experience and education, I have witnessed firsthand what *not* focusing on the Inner Game of Leadership costs people and companies.

But first, let's go back to one of my earliest memories as a five-year-old boy sitting in the backseat of my mom's Dodge Polara, my mom behind the steering wheel driving near our home in rural Michigan. She was arguing with one of her good friends, seated next to her in the front seat. As it got a bit heated in the subtle way discussions between two women get heated in the Midwest, I could see why they were disagreeing. It was crystal clear to me at age five but a mystery to them. The truth was: they thought they were disagreeing, but actually they *did* agree and were simply miscommunicating. I didn't yet know how to articulate what I saw; thus, what I tried to say to help them

3

didn't help. That experience has stuck with me because I could clearly see the communication issues that my mom and her friend could not see. I didn't know it at the time, but that early experience was indicative of the professional calling I would discover years later— executive coaching.

Fast-forward nearly five decades and I've seen many organizational difficulties stem from not recognizing and addressing the true root causes of people issues. Here are some of the poignant examples I've witnessed:

- Great people getting burned out and quitting their companies or, even worse, quitting in spirit without actually leaving
- High-functioning individuals coming together to form low-performing teams
- Inspiring company cultures go down in flames when financial pressures hit
- Wonderful leaders losing touch with the realities of the organizations they lead
- Well-meaning but unskilled leaders unintentionally demotivating their employees
- High-performing individuals getting promoted into leadership roles only to fail
- Misalignment between teams causing projects to fail
- Disempowerment of employees through micro-managing
- Good people withholding important – sometimes even critical – information from their bosses or peers for fear of retribution of some kind
- Organizational cultures that are more focused on turf-protecting than helping everyone be successful because they've forgotten that a rising tide lifts all boats
- Bullying behavior from people in power

Myles Munroe once said, "In the cemetery is buried the greatest treasure of untapped potential." So much more excellence, fulfillment, productivity, and profit are available to leaders and organizations. All we need to do is a better job of tapping into the full potential of the people in our organizations.

Hopefully you find these pithy anecdotes fun and perhaps even compelling. And like any good business person, you're probably also thinking *show me the data*. Fortunately, there is plenty of data to support the business value of mastering your Inner Game of Leadership. As you read this book, you will find data woven throughout, and let's get straight to it now with an introductory tour.

THE COSTS OF NOT FOCUSING ON THE INNER GAME OF LEADERSHIP

Consider that even amongst the highly educated and motivated workforce, some reports put team and organizational productivity at only 50% of capacity. This is largely due to communication breakdowns and trust issues. I've worked with hundreds of leaders and teams across disparate organizations, and one of the common themes is how high they often self-assess as to their overall team effectiveness. I still get surprised by this sometimes, but then I remind myself that few people have ever really experienced what a truly high-functioning team is: they simply don't know what they don't know. Just this one piece of information is astounding enough. Ask yourself this simple question: "What would become possible if I could double the productivity of my current staff?"

What's more, for years the US national average attrition rate has been about 20%, and some companies have experienced annual attrition rates in excess of 30%. The business impacts of COVID-19 in 2020 have created even more churn in the workforce. This all may seem like it's out of our control and just a sign of our current circumstances, but when people voluntarily leave a company, they primarily leave for push factors that have caused them to be unhappy in the first place. The most important push factor is their relationship with their immediate boss. As a case in point, one of our clients was able to reduce their annual attrition rate from a horrible 55% down to an industry-leading 10% by focusing primarily on leadership development. Thus, great leadership is often the greatest attractant of strong talent and the greatest catalyst for getting the most out of your talent, and poor leadership is often the greatest repellant of strong talent and a powerful de-motivating force.

Additionally, for many of today's companies that primarily employ white-collar workers, the hard costs alone of replacing an employee who quits is typically 50-250% of their annual compensation. Here's some quick, back-of-the-envelope math using just this one statistic: an organization of 1,000 employees, averaging $150,000 per year in total compensation with an average attrition rate of 20%, loses between $15,000,000 and $75,000,000 per year just to back-fill their staff. Even with a more conservative estimate of 10% attrition and an average compensation of only $75,000, we're still looking at somewhere between $3,750,000 to $18,750,000 per year. For additional data points using these assumptions, see figure 1.1.

Headcount	Attrition Per Year	Minimum Cost To Replace	Maximum Cost To Replace
500	100	$7,500,000	$37,500,000
1000	200	$15,000,000	$75,000,000
2500	500	$37,000,000	$187,500,000
5000	1000	$75,000,000	$375,000,000
10000	2000	$150,000,000	$750,000,000
25000	5000	$375,000,000	$1,875,000,000

Figure 1.1 – Cost of Employee Attrition

And that's just the hard costs associated with replacing employees. Those numbers do not account for the following related costs:

- Lost institutional knowledge reduces efficiency and productivity.
- Decreases in employee engagement when important people leave the company further reduce productivity.
- Lost productivity and increased burnout as others attempt to pick up the slack while a vacant position may require 6+ months to fill.

- Further lost productivity as it often takes 6-12 months for a newly hired employee to fully get up to speed.
- The best and highest-achieving people are often 4x, and sometimes as much as 10x, more productive than the average employee. When they leave, it *really* hurts.
- Your best performing people are also the most sought after by your competitors and often the most proactive about leaving for a better opportunity if they're unhappy.
- When a key person quits, they tend to take 2-3 other key people with them in the ensuing months.

Another important consideration is the organizational costs of poor employee engagement. Gallup has estimated that 17.2% of the US workforce is actively disengaged. These are people who are unhappy at work and acting out with behaviors like tardiness, missed workdays, and decreased productivity. Gallup estimates that each actively disengaged employee costs their organization 34% of that employee's annual compensation. If we again assume an organization of 1,000 employees averaging $150,000 per year in compensation, we can estimate that 172 of those employees are actively disengaged, and the total cost to the organization is $8,772,000 annually. See figure 1.2 for additional data points using these assumptions.

Additionally, some factors unaccounted for in Gallup's cost estimates of poor employee engagement are that actively disengaged employees are often sabotaging projects, interacting with customers in poor ways, and lowering the overall quality control of the organization.

Headcount	# Disengaged Employees	Estimated Cost of Disengaged Employees
500	86	$4,386,000
1000	172	$8,772,000
2500	430	$21,930,000
5000	860	$43,860,000
10000	1720	$87,720,000
25000	4300	$219,300,000

Figure 1.2 – Cost of Employee Disengagement

WHY EXECUTIVES STRUGGLE TO SEE THE BUSINESS VALUE OF MASTERING THE INNER GAME OF LEADERSHIP

Executives use metrics all the time to assess things like financial ratios, profits, margins, inventory, and customer satisfaction. Few executives these days would even think about running their businesses without key performance indicators like these informing their decisions. These traditional metrics are important. In many ways, they are the lifeblood of business. At the same time, they are dangerous. First, focusing on these metrics leaves out the less tangible people metrics that are not directly visible on any financial statement but are indirectly everywhere on all financial statements. Also, these metrics tend to focus our attention on outcomes more than what it takes to actually create the best outcomes—***people.***

Three of the biggest reasons senior executives tend to overly focus on non-people metrics are:

1. Metrics like financial ratios, profit, operational efficiencies, and customer satisfaction are all generally easier to quantify than softer metrics involving an organization's leadership, people, and culture.
2. There is often a large amount of pressure from investors (either private or public) to meet certain financial metrics in a timely fashion.
3. Executive compensation packages may reward short-term thinking over medium-to-long-term thinking.

Let's take a deeper look at the first motivation. We humans tend to take the path of least resistance often without being consciously aware that is what we are doing. Thus, with highly tangible and easily quantifiable metrics to focus on, it's easy to default to those metrics because they feel more understandable, more controllable, and more immediate than the difficult-to-quantify, "softer," and seemingly more difficult to control metrics about the people and culture of the organization.

The second motivation is largely the result of a bigger, systemic issue, at least within the United States, where shareholders and Chief Financial Officers (CFOs) tend to get too much airtime in executive decision-making compared to Chief People Officers (CPOs), Chief Human Resources Officers (CHROs), and Chief Learning Officers (CLOs). As one salient example, I've held a number of executive roundtable discussions in Silicon Valley where I've brought together a small cadre of CHROs, CPOs, and CLOs behind closed doors to discuss this very issue and strategize together about how they can influence executive decision-making to better account for people and culture. Even in the Silicon Valley area, which is renowned for the high value companies place on their people and cultures, CFOs often have an inordinate influence on executive leadership decisions compared to their counterparts who are experts in people, learning, and culture.

The third motivation is driven by the culture, at least here in the United States, where senior executives and CEOs in particular are sometimes compensated in ways that run counter to the greater good of the organization. It is also influenced by shareholders and a tendency to make heroes out of CEOs and sometimes compensate them inordinately.

Thus, senior executives are often faced with a cognitive bias in favor of metrics that feel easier, a large amount of pressure from shareholders (and by extension the CFO), and an incentive package that may be rewarding the wrong behaviors. These three factors are major contributors to why senior executives commonly focus too much of their attention on financial levers, strategy levers, and operational efficiency levers.

Every single one of these metrics and levers depends entirely on leadership, people, culture, and teamwork. It's simply impossible to have great profits, products, or processes without a highly productive, inspired, and engaged team that is vigorously and purposefully rowing in the same direction every single day.

THE CALL TO ACTION

In the leadership race of the 21st century, we must adapt to lead more relationally, or we will be left behind. The culture of any organization is set by the example of the leadership in that organization and nowhere more so than the highest-ranking leaders. Some say that culture eats strategy for breakfast. In my experience, that is too soft of a statement. I believe it is more accurate to say that culture eats everything in its path, so you'd better send it in the right direction. As an executive coach working with executive leadership teams across the world, I am astounded by how quickly executive teams will sometimes turn to re-organization as the answer to their communication, profitability, and cultural issues. A well-done reorganization can be a very effective change tool, but too many leaders end up reorganizing in a change-du-jour kind of way which too often undermines morale, trust, and culture.

When I work with leaders on culture change, I advise them to think in timelines of at least 18-24 months to see tangible improvements from that change initiative. When I see any leadership team re-organizing more often than that, I see a leadership team that is likely in trouble. It is often a sign the senior leadership team isn't willing to take a hard look inside themselves; the team isn't willing to assess who they're being, what they're modeling, how they are leading –and thereby the culture *they* are creating—as the source of their challenges.

At the same time, if we aren't one of the executive leaders operating at the highest levels of an organization, we cannot simply point our fingers at "them" as the only source of the problem. What we have the most control over is ourselves: how we show up, how we lead, and the example we set. As Gandhi once said, "You must be the change you want to see in the world." I will be the first to admit that inner transformation isn't everything. It needs to be applied through consistent and persistent action before sustainable change can be affected. But if we haven't done our inner work to be the change we want to see in the world, we are less likely to succeed in influencing anyone else to change. That's because people often pay more attention to what we do and who we are being than to what we say.

It feels like a paradox, but a basic fact of peak human performance is that we get better results and perform more optimally when we're not overly focused on the outcome. Instead, if we focus on hitting the marks that we know will drive us toward the best possible outcome and then surrender to whatever happens when we give it our very best, we are more likely to win. Winning, by definition, is not completely under our control because it involves other people who might be better than we are that day. What is under our control is being the best possible version of ourselves every minute of every day in service to maximizing the chances that we **will** win.

Simply put, in today's world if we cannot lead ourselves first, we cannot lead anyone else. With the rise of technology and a much more interconnected world, the lines between our work lives and private lives have become completely blurred for many of us. As I'm writing this in December of 2020, that has never been more true. For most of 2020, the COVID-19 pandemic has caused many of us to work from home full-time while also working harder than ever. While more people will return to the office as we get COVID-19 under better control, there's every indication that technology and modern life are heading more and more in this always-on direction. Yet, despite being more connected to the rest of the world than ever before via social media, texting, smartphones, tablets, etc., we report feeling lonelier than we've ever felt before. That's because we've lost touch with the most precious and important leadership relationship of all – the one we have with ourselves.

Given the new always-on normal, it has never been more important to deepen our relationship with ourselves. Only from a rock-solid foundation of inner drive, resilience, and wisdom can we truly thrive as a leader in this new VUCA world. From that rock-solid core comes an unshakeable sense of self, purpose, and autonomy. Emotional triggers, distractions, and insatiable demands on our time no longer pull us off track. They simply become the quiet noise of circumstance while we stay more centered and grounded in our most powerful leadership self.

Pointing the finger of responsibility elsewhere, however "right" we might be, only diminishes our power to change our lives for the better. If we're not focused on the biggest bang for the buck places (in this case – **ourselves**), then it doesn't matter how hard we work. We might be running our motors at redline (and beyond), but if we're headed for the concrete wall on the side of the racetrack instead of the apex of the next corner, we're just going to crash and burn that much harder.

Chapter 2

Your Sighting Lap for the Race of Your Life

JUST BEFORE EVERY MOTORCYCLE race, the racers are given a "sighting" lap, a lap which is taken at slower-than-race speeds. Sighting laps give racers a chance to mentally prepare for the race that is about to start. They enable them to see and experience the current racetrack conditions and, thereby, be fully prepared for when the green flag drops and the race begins.

This chapter is meant to serve as a sighting lap for the new leadership journey we are about to embark on. To master our Inner Game of Leadership, we must be willing to do the following.

Do the Difficult Inner Work of Being a Great Leader

When you think of examples of what it takes to be the best leader you can be, who do you think of? Give yourself a moment to reflect on this and jot down some answers.

When I ask this question of clients, I often get answers like Steve Jobs, Elon Musk, Gandhi, Martin Luther King, John Wooden, Mandela, Jeff Bezos, Warren Buffet, Bog Iger, Reed Hastings, Bill Gates, Sheryl Sandberg, etc.

But the most effective answer to this question is *you*.

Be the best version of you. The world doesn't need another Steve Jobs, and you cannot possibly be him anyway. When we try to emulate a leader we admire, our presence doesn't ring true to others. They may not consciously know why, but they trust us less because we're not being ourselves. Instead, we're trying to be someone we're not. Remember: people pay more attention to who we are and what we do than what we say.

In the leadership arena, the word "authenticity" is overused. What does authenticity really mean in a leadership context? For the purposes of this book, what it means is to be the best and most effective leadership version of *you*. While we can and should learn from others who have come before us, the place to look is inside ourselves. **Everyone** has the capacity to be a great leader. We just have to be willing to do the inner work.

I believe that too many people assume leadership is either something you are born with or not born with. While it is true that some people have a genetic make-up and/or a childhood environment that better prepared them for leadership, the best leaders didn't get there without a lot of hard work in the form of failure, introspection, personal growth, and constant learning about themselves and the world they live in.

Natural ability is overrated and, to a significant degree, is a fairy tale. If we look closely at anyone who has reached the upper echelons of any endeavor, they only got there through dedication to their craft and consistent practice – even (or especially) when it felt difficult. I agree with award-winning author/journalist Malcom Gladwell that it takes about 10,000 hours of practice to master anything, including leadership. But it's not just 10,000 hours in the job; it's 10,000 hours of **mindful** practice. The fact is that many of the people who have some genetic and/or environmental gifts for leadership take it for granted and often don't strive to improve themselves enough. It's the people who put in the mindful practice and continually and relentlessly focus on living outside their comfort zone in order to grow and improve that overtake and dominate in leadership; it is not the ones who have natural ability but forego the inner work.

We, you, and the universe all need more mindful and authentic leaders. No one gets there without a commitment to their own inner work. We can't control whatever genetics we were born with. We can't go back in time and change our childhood for the better. We *can* control our work ethic. Our authentic and unique leadership presence can only blossom by mastering our Inner Game of Leadership.

DISRUPT YOURSELF BEFORE YOU ARE DISRUPTED

Whether we like it or not, the world is changing rapidly, and positional authority – or what some might call command-and-control leadership - doesn't carry the weight it used to. Relational authority – influence – is the more powerful and reliable paradigm in our VUCA world. But transitioning to be more relationship-focused is a key challenge for many leaders. To adopt the new paradigm, we must first break free of our current paradigm. If we don't get ahead of the curve, the curve will get ahead of us, and we are then much more likely to be catastrophically disrupted in our careers.

Leaders often begin work with me as their executive coach for what I call surface reasons. This is because the reasons they self-diagnose are often just underlying symptoms of bigger issues. One of the common surface issues is that they've been unexpectedly passed over for a big promotion or perhaps even laid off or fired. Many of us think that won't happen to us, but the fact is that change and adaptation are a part of leadership and life. If we don't continually grow ahead of the change that is coming, that growth will likely be forced upon us in the form of a painful disruption like a layoff or missed promotion. Additionally, ambitious individuals looking to move up will eventually be promoted to their level of incompetence. This was well researched by Laurence J. Peter and Raymond Hull in their book, *The Peter Principle*. Marshall Goldsmith has also written about this topic in his book, *What Got You Here, Won't Get You There*.

Many leaders we work with have reached a point in their careers where they need to let go of what they think they know. This can take many different forms, but a common struggle for many leaders is transitioning from being an amazing individual contributor who gets stuff done to being a great executive leader who gets stuff done through others. In many organizations, high achievers get promoted into leadership roles without knowing enough about how to lead. They somehow stumble through it, learn some things along the way, and get by OK for a period of time. However, a time comes when they begin to struggle to meet expectations and they don't understand why.

More often than not, what is needed is to transition into more relationship-based leadership and to let go of direct control and, instead, focus exclusively on getting stuff done through others. It's the only way to scale ourselves (i.e. to achieve organizational goals through others in a multiplicative way) as leaders. No matter how much of a superman or superwoman we might be, we're just one person in a much larger organization. Being a star achiever is actually the exact opposite of what a truly great leader needs to focus on. Few leaders are able to make this transition alone because it often goes against the grain of everything they've been rewarded for in their career progression.

If the tumultuous year of 2020 taught us anything, it is that the only constant in life is change. We're meant to be learning, growing, and evolving. We need to be focused on proactively disrupting ourselves in order to be ready for our next level of growth and achievement. If we don't, we're likely in for more painful career disruptions, missed opportunities, and limited advancement in our careers and lives.

Disruption *will* happen to you. Would you rather be prepared by disrupting yourself consciously and proactively, or be surprised and on your heels by the next set of VUCA disruptions? And the next set after that? And the next?? VUCA is here to stay, so it behooves us to learn how to thrive in today's VUCA world by mastering our Inner Game of Leadership.

TREAT MASTERING YOUR INNER GAME OF LEADERSHIP LIKE A BIG ROCK

Relentlessly focusing our attention on only the most important things in our life can be challenging, but it is a crucial skill to master if we are to become unshakeable in our influence.

A proverbial story illustrating the importance of this skill goes something like this:

One day an expert was speaking to a group of overachieving business students. He pulled out an empty, gallon-size, clear glass jar and set it on the podium in front of him. Then he silently produced about a dozen big rocks and placed them, one at a time, into the jar.

When the jar was filled to the top and no more rocks would fit inside, he asked, "Is this jar full?"

Everyone said, "Yes." He replied, "Really?" and proceeded to pull out a bag of pebbles and dump them into the jar. He shook the jar, causing the pebbles to fall into all the spaces between the big rocks, then added more pebbles until the jar appeared to be full again.

He then asked the students again, "Is this jar full now?"

The students were beginning to catch on. "Probably not," one of them answered.

"Very good!" he replied. He then pulled out a bucket of sand. He dumped sand into the jar, and it went into all the remaining spaces between the rocks and the pebbles. Then he asked, "Is this jar full?"

"No!" the class shouted.

"Excellent!" he replied. Then he grabbed a pitcher of water and poured it in until the jar was filled to the brim.

The teacher looked intently back at the students and asked, "What is the point of this exercise?"

One student immediately and proudly proclaimed, "The point is that no matter how full your schedule is, if you try really hard, you can always fit more in!"

"No," the expert replied, "The truth illustrated by this exercise is that if you don't put the big rocks in first, you will never get them in at all."

What this story tells us is that we must consciously fill our lives with our big rocks (the most important things) first, or else the pebbles, sand, and water of our lives (the less important things) will effectively crowd out the most important things.

If I had $100 for every time I've heard leaders tell me they don't have time to do the inner work of being a great leader, I'd be a wealthy man. My answer to this statement is always the same: we simply don't have time **not** to do the inner work. This is because when we do our inner work well enough, we will be able to navigate our day-to-day VUCA leadership existence in a whole new way that feels easier, is less stressful, and most importantly, is more effective and drives better business results.

The inner work of being a great leader is a big rock. It will always be a big rock. In fact, it may be the biggest rock of all, and we need to deliberately and proactively treat it as such, or else it will get crowded out by the pebbles, sand, and water in our lives.

SLOW DOWN IN ORDER TO GO FASTER

To master your Inner Game of Leadership, you will need to slow down in order to go faster.

It may seem counter-intuitive, but in motorcycle road-racing, a common rookie mistake is to enter corners too fast. Rookies don't know any better and typically assume the trick to being a fast racer is to immediately go as fast as possible everywhere on the racetrack. This is a mistake because the fastest path around a racetrack is to arc each corner in such a way that we hit the exit of each corner with maximum speed. Arcing a corner in this way is typically a longer path than is strictly necessary. It also typically involves entering the corner more slowly to maximize corner exit speed. But taking the longer path and using slower entry speed pay off in a big way because the fastest path on the racetrack is to maximize your exit speed from the corner. In racing vernacular, riding the fastest path on the racetrack (instead of the most direct path) is commonly called "the racing line" or simply "the line."

This is most easily shown with an illustration. Figure 2.1 shows turn 11 at Sonoma Raceway in Northern California. Turn 11 is a slow, right-hand, 180-degree corner. This corner is a pretty classic racetrack corner in that you need to go slower on the entry to maximize your exit. It is also a dangerous corner because there is no room for error at the exit of the corner—there is a concrete wall right at the edge of the track.

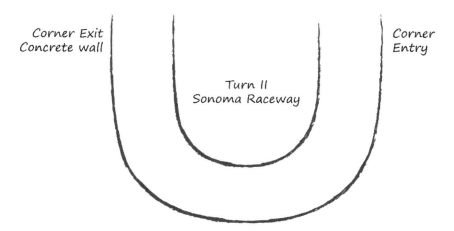

Figure 2.1 – Turn 11 at Sonoma Raceway

In figure 2.2 you can see the line that a rookie will choose through this corner. This line will require the rookie to slow down at the exit of the corner to avoid hitting the wall, thereby reducing the exit speed from the corner and worsening his lap time. This is because he's turned into the corner too early and also because he entered the corner with too much speed.

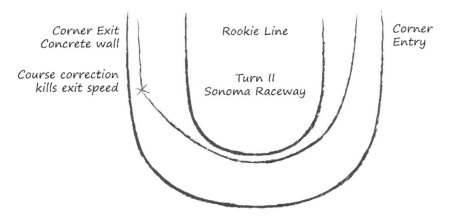

Figure 2.2 – Rookie Line Through Turn 11 at Sonoma Raceway

In figure 2.3 you can see the line that an experienced racer will choose. This line will allow the racer to maximize their exit speed from the corner because it doesn't have them aimed at the concrete wall when exiting, but rather it has them aimed up the straightaway. This is the result of having entered the corner a bit slower and also of having turned into the corner a bit later. This is the kind of line that a racer must choose in every corner to have any chance at winning races.

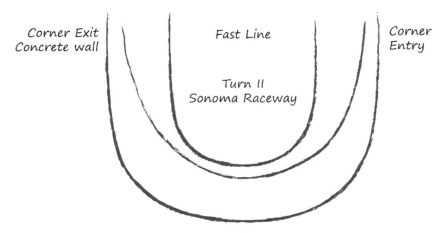

Figure 2.3 – Fast Line Through Turn 11 at Sonoma Raceway

Thus, as rookie racers gain more experience, they actually slow down their entry speed into each corner to learn to turn into the corner later in order to hit the apex of each corner just right. Once they have mastered their lines through each corner, then they can increase their speed and find themselves going much faster and doing so more safely! This is where the saying in motorcycle racing comes from, that you need to "slow down in order to go faster." A rookie racer must learn to do this in each and every corner in order to have any chance of winning.

So what does all this have to do with mastering your Inner Game of Leadership? Right now, you're more like that rookie racer. You probably feel like you're already going about as fast as you can go. How could you possibly go any faster? The fact is, just like that rookie motorcycle racer, you are going as fast as you can for the line you've chosen, *but you've chosen the wrong line because you don't know what you don't know.*

To go faster as a leader, you will first have to slow down and re-learn how to lead. Initially, mastering your Inner Game of Leadership will slow you down because there is a ramp-up time in any learning curve. However, you will get your time back very soon, and then your time gain will be multiplied for years to come as you go deeper into mastering your Inner Game of Leadership.

With the leaders we coach 1:1, typically around three to four months into the process they start to get their time back in a multiplicative way. That is when they begin to become more effective and efficient and experience less stress, more ease, and more confidence. That is when they become considerably better at achieving results by influencing others to do their best work. The best part is that, in exchange for slowing down for only three to four months, they get a lifetime of going faster and doing it with more ease. A similar return on investment is available to you with this book.

GET COMFORTABLE BEING UNCOMFORTABLE

You may sometimes feel uncomfortable reading this book. That is a good thing because change does not happen without discomfort.

When it comes to learning and improving, our comfort zone is the enemy.

At the same time, comfort is good. We sometimes need it to feel safe. People often function at their best when they can spend a portion of their time in their comfort zone. Our comfort zone soothes us and helps us feel that the world is predictable and not too stressful. Unfortunately, we can grow addicted to the comfort of the familiar. Our comfort zone can become too comfortable and leave us craving comfort while trying to change – an oxymoron that is the primary reason why so many change initiatives (whether personal or organizational) fail.

Think of a body-builder or any athlete at the top of their game. They spend hours and hours training their bodies to strengthen muscles, build agility, habituate the precise physical form, strengthen their mental focus, and build their "heart" to be able to dig deep when it really counts. No top athlete would expect themselves to perform at the top of their game and get the opportunity to shoot the game-winning basket without all of those hours and hours of training. And guess what? That training often doesn't feel comfortable. They're stretching their bodies and minds beyond their limits by staying in their learning zone, the zone of mental, emotional, and physical discomfort, much longer than they ever imagined was possible.

Why would any leader expect themselves to perform at their best or get the opportunity for that next big promotion without doing the inner work of learning, growing, and stretching themselves every day?

The difference between top performers in leadership and everyone else is their willingness to get more comfortable being uncomfortable. They push themselves beyond their perceived limits, every single day. And here's the thing: we're really not meant to remain comfortable in life. Comfort is only where we rest. Discomfort is synonymous with learning and growing. If we choose to stay in our comfort zone all the time, we're choosing to live a dull and toned-down version of our life.

If we want to master our Inner Game of Leadership, we must choose to live in our learning zone and only visit our comfort zone when we need to rest.

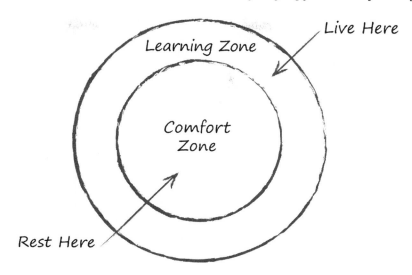

Figure 2.4 – Comfort Zone and Learning Zone

RECOGNIZE THAT CHANGE IS HARD, AND DO IT ANYWAY

Improvement does not happen without change. I like to say that change is both deceptively easy and deceptively difficult at the same time. It is deceptively easy from the technical standpoint. Doing something different than you have done before is just a matter of making a different decision and taking a different action. Make a different decision, take a different action—change is complete. Conceptually, it's simple.

Yet our brains are masterful at wiring our neurons together in such a way that thoughts, feelings, and behaviors become automatic. Anyone who has been driving a car for a significant number of years has likely had the experience of arriving at their destination completely safe and sound while having no conscious memory of having made the drive. Our minds work this way so that we can be freed up for higher-order thinking. Unconscious habitual thoughts, feelings, and behaviors feel comfortable and easy. That is a wonderful thing because if *everything* we did required our conscious attention, we'd be overwhelmed in a microsecond.

Changing habits, including habits of thought, feeling, and behavior, requires much conscious effort, and your mind is likely to resist that change in the form of making you feel uncomfortable as you try adopting new habits. But every one of your automatic habitual thoughts, feelings, and behaviors once required your complete, conscious attention. It's only by repeating those thoughts, feelings, and behaviors again and again that they became automatic and no longer required conscious effort. Since you've done it before, you can certainly do it again.

Another key problem with making changes in our life is that our brains are wired to overvalue the status quo. One great, illustrative example of our innate status quo bias is to look at the differences in organ donor rates between countries that require citizens to opt-out of being an organ donor (like Austria) and countries that require citizens to opt-in (like the United States). In Austria, the organ donor rate is more than 90%. In the United States, it is less than 15%. When faced with a decision that we're not immediately sure how to answer, we will nearly always go with the status quo, or default status.

The field of behavioral economics has also uncovered a number of other irrational biases that play into our status quo bias—the endowment effect, for example. The endowment effect, essentially, is our propensity to ascribe a higher value to something simply because we already own it. In my Executive MBA program at Columbia Business School, I was able to experience firsthand one of the most repeatable studies ever done on the endowment effect.

On the first day of class, our behavioral economics professor randomly distributed a Columbia coffee mug to half of the students in the course; the other half of the students received nothing. This was immediately followed by an anonymous survey. Those students who had received a free mug were asked, "What is the lowest dollar amount for which you'd be willing to sell the mug?" Those students who did not receive a free mug were asked, "What is the highest dollar amount you'd be willing to pay to purchase the mug?" Those who had received the free mug wanted $8 on average to sell it, and those who didn't receive a mug would only pay $4 on average to purchase one. And only minutes beforehand, no one had any mugs at all!

Our resistance to change is also related to our survival instinct. In the short term, if we do things the way we've always done them, we are more likely to survive another day. If our behavior kept us alive yesterday, there's a very good chance it will keep us alive today. In the long term though, micro-changes that seem like nothing by themselves can eventually add up to disaster. Our brains are mostly trained to see the immediacy of a tiger hunting us, and we immediately react accordingly, thereby maximizing our chances of survival. Our brains are much less trained to see, accept, and avert the slow incremental changes that can also lead to bad consequences and even death. Global warming is one example of this.

At the end of the day, we are wired to follow the path of least resistance. If it feels difficult, is not immediately rewarding nor immediately threatening to our livelihood, it's easy for us to default to doing nothing different from what we've done previously.

For that reason, change can feel both deceptively easy and deceptively difficult at the same time. Conceptually, habit change is simple. But when we're stuck in old habits and lack knowledge, perseverance, and effective tools to change those habits, change can feel near impossible.

We've walked through a number of the key factors that make change difficult. To bring it all together in a simple model, the difficulty of making sustainable behavioral change can be summed up rather nicely by what is commonly called the Valley of Despair (see figure 2.5). This model applies to any change initiative of any scale, ranging from an individual's New Year's resolution to a large-scale culture change initiative of epic proportions - and everything in between. The Valley of Despair inevitably comes into play with any change initiative, sometimes many times and in different variations.

Change: The Valley of Despair

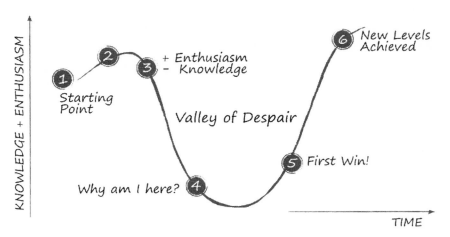

Figure 2.5 – Valley of Despair

Some studies suggest that about 70% of culture change initiatives fail to meet expectations. Another study says that 91% of New Year's resolutions fail. When behavior changes fail, the primary cause is nothing more than giving up before achieving the goal. And when we do give up, it's nearly always at or near the bottom of the Valley of Despair (see point 4 on figure 2.5). By definition, when we're near the bottom of the valley, we cannot see or even envision a path forward. We feel stuck, question why we ever believed this change was "worth it" or a good idea, and we may even feel hopeless that the change will ever work anyway. This is when the danger of giving up is at its highest. Once we give up, we snap back to point 1 on the diagram and probably convince ourselves the change initiative was a bad idea anyway.

What we need at that difficult crux point at the bottom of the Valley of Despair is motivation to keep going even when it feels difficult – perhaps incredibly difficult and hopeless. If we keep going, we are likely to achieve our first big win (point 5 on the diagram), and an upward spiral to point 6 (success!) is likely to be achieved. The thing is: at the bottom of the pit, our minds will have a difficult time seeing any reasonable path forward. It's usually not that there isn't a path forward; we just can't see it.

The most effective way to counteract the negative Mindset that coincides with the crux point on the valley is to proactively create a plan for how you will reconnect with your motivation to keep going when it gets difficult. It is important to focus on reconnecting with the *why* behind the change, why it's important to you, and *how it will feel* when you've reached your goal. After you've done that, you then want to proactively create specific accountability strategies to help you persevere when you hit the crux point at the bottom of the Valley of Despair.

In the context of mastering your Inner Game of Leadership, it is important to take some time now to get really clear about why this is important to you. Here are some questions to get you started:

- Why does mastering my Inner Game of Leadership matter to me?
- What excites me about mastering my Inner Game of Leadership?
- What will it emotionally feel like to live my life with unshakeable influence? Why is it important for me to feel that way?
- What will happen to my level of fulfillment in life when I am more masterful with my Inner Game of Leadership?
- What financial payoffs are likely in store for me as I become more unshakeable in my influence?
- What is the payoff to my team when I succeed? What benefits will they experience?
- What is the payoff to my company when I succeed? What benefits will they experience?

Now, take some time to create a system of motivation and accountability that you can rely on when it gets effortful. First, while you're still excited about mastering your Inner Game of Leadership, write a motivational letter to your future self that is stuck at the bottom of the Valley of Despair. Perhaps there have been some unexpected setbacks that have you feeling down; perhaps it's taking longer than you would like and you're getting impatient; perhaps you are seriously questioning why you ever believed you could do it.

Try to imagine the future rationalizations that you are likely to come up with. With those in mind, write to your future self now in a motivational way to overcome those obstacles and keep going.

An important point about writing this letter is to make sure you write it from the point of view of what you **do** want, not what you **don't** want. For example, instead of writing, "Don't give up," write "Keep going" or "You can do this." As another example, instead of writing, "Failure is not an option," write "Success is mine if I persevere."

Once you've written the letter, seal it in an envelope, then write "MY MOTIVATION" or "MY WHY" across the front and put it in your desk in a prominent location where you will see it often. When persistence becomes difficult and you want to give up, open the letter and read it. Then re-read it as often as you need to in order to stay motivated.

Next, now that you have a clear sense of why this is important to you and what your motivation for this change is, you want to enlist some of your colleagues into your success. Socializing your commitments with people you like and respect is one of the most reliable ways to keep yourself on track when mastering your Inner Game of Leadership gets hard. It's often best that it not be a good friend or family member. Good friends and family members sometimes let us off the hook too easily. It's best to enlist people that know you, respect you, and want you to succeed but are not so close to you that they might let you slide.

Believe it or not, one of the more effective strategies some executives we've worked with have used is to enlist one of their office rivals in this way! For some people, the fear of one of their rivals knowing that they gave up is a huge motivation to persevere when it gets hard. Whoever you enlist in your success, you want to have regular check-in conversations with them where you update them on your progress and they keep you accountable to moving forward. This kind of buddy system is one of the more reliable ways I've seen to ensure success in pushing through the Valley of Despair.

LET GO OF YOUR NEVER-ENDING CYCLE OF REACTIVITY

In the years that I've been coaching leaders, I've noticed a pattern of reactivity that many carry, which I call the never-ending cycle of reactivity. Some have this pattern of thought, feeling, and behavior more than others, but nearly everyone has it. To illustrate this seemingly never-ending cycle of reactivity, figure 2.6 shows how we tend to overreact. The dotted line represents the reality of our circumstances. The solid line represents the magnitude of our emotional reaction to our circumstances. As you can see, the tendency is to strongly overreact with emotional highs and emotional lows that are out of proportion to reality. This tendency is one of the bigger obstacles leaders face in mastering their Inner Game of Leadership. In times of great change, turmoil, and stress, like many of us experienced in 2020, our tendency to over-react becomes even more problematic to mastering our Inner Game of Leadership.

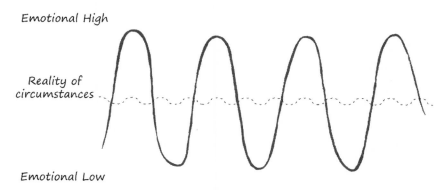

Figure 2.6 – Reactivity Model

You may be triggered and have reactions while reading this book. In fact, whether we know it consciously or not, we are being emotionally triggered much of the time. About 70-80% of all adults live primarily in a reactive Mindset, and those who don't are still in a reactive Mindset a significant portion of the time. That reactive Mindset has us responding to our lives based on fear.

In case you're not clear if this applies to you, ask yourself some questions:

- Do you get upset in any way after someone cuts you off in traffic?
- Do you get upset when your boss tells you what you are doing wrong?
- Do you get upset when a colleague takes credit for your work?
- Do you get upset when your romantic partner interrupts you when you're speaking?
- Do you get upset with your child for not doing as they're told?

These are all emotional triggers, and they are running our thoughts, feelings, and behaviors more than we know. The example behaviors listed above are not the best behaviors, and we don't have to accept them. What we do need to accept is that our emotional reactions to others' behavior cloud our vision, drive our stress levels up, kick our body into the fight-or-flight response, and contribute to us communicating and leading in a less effective way.

All emotional triggers are based on fear. Some examples are:

- The fear that you don't matter
- The fear that you will be passed over for promotion again
- The fear that your voice won't be heard
- The fear of failure
- The fear that you won't get your needs met in any fashion

We are actually born with only two fears: the fear of falling and the fear of loud noises. All other fears are learned and, therefore, can be unlearned. Some learned fears serve us well, like the fear of burning our hand on a hot stove. But many leadership fears operate on a largely unconscious level and hold us back.

As one key example, the fear of failure is a universal fear that nearly every leader we work with suffers from, so we lead them through a process to learn how to welcome failure as a necessary part of their learning on their way to success. Further, we talk about how failure is a Mindset, not an outcome. As a key example of failure being a Mindset rather than an outcome, Thomas Edison is credited as having said that he did not fail 1,000 times before successfully creating the incandescent light bulb, he succeeded in proving that those 1,000 ways of building a light bulb did not work before finding a way that did work. In other words, all those "failures" were actually successful and necessary learning steps on his way to inventing the light bulb. If he had stopped after 999 attempts because he fell into a Mindset of failure, the world would be a different place today.

If there is any such thing as failure, I would define it as giving up before meeting our goals. If a goal is truly important to us, why would we ever give up before achieving it? History is brimming with stories of impossible goals being achieved because people believed it was possible and didn't give up before achieving the goal.

Watching my son learn how to walk was a great learning experience for me. It took him countless tries. Like any child, he banged himself up along the learning curve, but he relentlessly pursued his goal of learning how to walk regardless of the falls and scrapes along the way. Then later he did the same with learning how to run and how to speak. While he did sometimes get frustrated, angry, or sad in response to setbacks, he never got so overrun by any emotional reaction that he gave up entirely.

An emotional reaction, by definition, is based on our past experiences. When our amygdala interprets our current circumstances as being similar enough to a past emotional wound, it triggers a fight-or-flight response – and we're off to the races of emotional reactivity. The thing is: our brain's mechanism for protecting us by overlaying our past emotional wounds onto our current circumstances is imperfect and often triggers emotional reactions that are disproportionate – maybe even highly disproportionate – to the current circumstances. A key part of the work of mastering our Inner Game of Leadership is learning how to let go of this never-ending cycle of reactivity and drama by re-training our minds.

Fears will surface in various ways as we work through the process of mastering our Inner Game of Leadership. If they don't, we're staying in our comfort zone too much and not giving ourselves the opportunity to grow. When fear arises, we have the opportunity to make different choices in our present circumstances, thereby beginning to let go of old fears by giving ourselves a new experience.

Fears that drive our reactivity are unlikely to dissipate quickly. We need to be willing to do things despite our fear. Slowly over time that fear is likely to dissipate as our amygdala realizes (through actual new experiences, not just new thoughts) that we are safe making different choices and taking different action than we have in the past. Nothing will change for us as leaders until we take new and different actions than we've taken before. And we can't do that if we allow our irrational fears and the reactivity that stems from them to run our lives.

This is one of the most beautiful things about the Inner Game of Leadership. When we begin to master our reactivity and thereby learn how to respond to our circumstances in more conscious, creative, and effective ways, we will experience a new level of inner calm, groundedness, and confidence that we may not even be able to imagine yet.

Ram Dass said, "You cannot suffer the past or the future. What you are suffering is your memory and your imagination." Our never-ending cycle of reactivity is like a roller coaster ride of our own invention. Our triggers put us into a reactive state of fear. We then use our imagination from that place of reactive fear to create a distorted projection of what we imagine will happen in the future. We also use our distorted memory of the past to fuel our distorted interpretation of what is happening now.

When we get far enough along in our mastery of the Inner Game of Leadership, the circumstances of our leadership life will feel more and more like what they actually are—just neutral information. Any emotional charge we have around our circumstances will become subtler and less likely to overtake our conscious mind. We will be able to respond from our best leadership self more often.

PART 2

Mindset

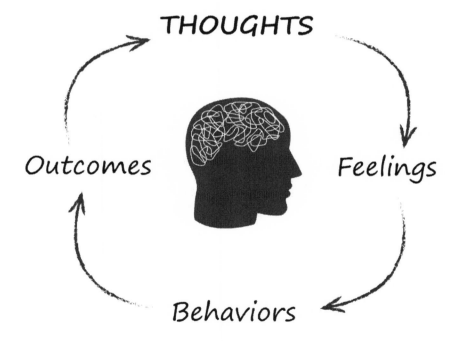

Mindset Definition:
Our established set of beliefs and attitudes and the habitual thoughts
we have about ourselves and the world.

Chapter 3

Introduction to Mindset

THERE'S A SAYING IN motorcycle racing that, "You go where you look." The idea is that if you focus your vision on the concrete wall on the side of the racetrack, that's exactly where your motorcycle will tend to go—whether you like it or not! And if you focus your attention on hitting the apex of the next corner just right so you can get the best possible lap time, then that's what your motorcycle will tend to do.

One of the most compelling racetrack examples of this played out in front of me as I was racing at Buttonwillow Raceway on a hot summer day in central California in the year 2000. In a 60-mph corner called "the bus stop," a racer crashed less than 100 feet ahead of me. His motorcycle and body went off the racetrack and into the dirt and immediately started tumbling in a spectacular way. There was one racer in between the crashed rider and me. That racer instinctively focused his vision on the tumbling motorcycle and body. In doing so, he very quickly (yet unconsciously) took his motorcycle off the racetrack and into the dirt, and he crashed too. While all this was happening, I consciously focused my vision where I wanted to go – the apex of the corner – and not only avoided crashing but didn't even lose any speed. I ended up finishing that race in 7th place, my best finish yet.

The concept that you go where you look applies everywhere in life and nowhere more so than with our leadership Mindset. As a leader, if our Mindset is focused on the wrong things, we will limit our performance and the performance of those around us. If we focus on the right things, we will multiply our own performance and the performance of those around us. What's more, the business impact of positive thinking is not just conjecture or a feel-good exercise. The idea that thinking positively creates more positive outcomes is a well-understood and well-researched phenomena in the world of positive psychology.

In his groundbreaking and best-selling book, *The Happiness Advantage*, positive psychology expert Shawn Achor highlights a study of entry-level accountants. The study found that the accountants who believed they could accomplish what they set out to do were the ones who were rated the highest on their performance reviews a year later. Here's the kicker from this study: *The accountants' belief in their ability had a bigger effect on their ratings than their actual skill level measured at the beginning of the year.*

In another study, prior to the beginning of the school year, elementary school teachers were told that specific students had been tested and shown to be academic superstars. The teachers were told that these were the students with the greatest potential for growth. By the end of the school year, these children's results showed that they were, in fact, academic superstars. However, the researchers had actually chosen these children at random and lied to the teachers about how they had tested. These children had actually tested as completely ordinary in their abilities. Simply through the teachers' belief in them, they had become extraordinary.

And finally, in his *Harvard Business Review* article entitled "Positive Intelligence," Shawn Achor states, "Research shows that when people work with a positive mindset, performance on nearly every level – productivity, creativity, engagement – improves."

Positive psychology is a relatively new field of study, and the body of research is growing rapidly. Already, many empirical studies are demonstrating the power of positive thinking on outcomes. The examples shared here are just a few of the poignant ones. If you want to learn more on this topic, you may want to start with Shawn Achor's TED talk then read his aforementioned book.

In addition to positive psychology, neuroscience research is advancing rapidly. Up until the last few decades, researchers believed that our brain's ability to learn, grow and change slowed way down when our brains reached their full physical maturity at around age 25. This created the commonly held beliefs that children can learn easily and adults struggle to learn anything new.

However, recent studies of neuroplasticity suggest otherwise. For example, in her book *Mindset*, Carol Dweck, Professor of Psychology at Stanford University, makes important distinctions between a growth mindset and a fixed mindset. A growth mindset is essentially the belief that we can improve our skills when we apply ourselves. This mindset leads to people making changes and improvement at all ages. A fixed mindset is the belief that our skills and abilities are innate and fixed in nature. This mindset inhibits any change or improvement in ourselves. In short, if we believe we can change and improve, then we will change and improve, and if we think we can't, then we won't. Or as Henry Ford succinctly stated, "If you think you can do a thing or you think you can't do a thing, you're right."

Now that we've laid the groundwork to establish the power of our Mindset on business outcomes, let's take a deeper look at how our Mindset pertains to mastering our Inner Game of Leadership.

META-THINKING

Few leaders give much consideration to meta-thinking, i.e. thinking about how we think, but it is one of the most important happiness, fulfillment, and productivity hacks on the planet. For instance, in her book *The How of Happiness*, psychology professor Sonja Lyubomirsky makes the empirically based argument that happiness is determined by three primary factors: our genetics, our life circumstances, and our Mindset—how we internally interpret and make sense of our life circumstances. This makes intuitive sense. The surprising part is this: about 50% of our happiness level is caused by our genetics, and only 10% is based on our life circumstances. Thus, 40% of our happiness is based on our Mindset.

Think about that for a moment... the vast majority of us focus the bulk of our time and energy on controlling the circumstances of our life in the false belief that it will be a major factor in making us happier. The truth is: focusing our energy on our Mindset – the stories we tell ourselves about who we are, who we are not, and how the world works – is 4x more powerful at making us happy than focusing on our life circumstances.

Most importantly, studies show that we do our best work, are the most creative, productive, engaged, and fulfilled when we are happy. And since we as humans tend to mirror each other's emotions, happiness is contagious to those around us. Thus, as we become happier, we tend to create an upward spiral of increased happiness, productivity, and effectiveness on all others we influence. Focusing on improving our Mindset is one of the most powerful tools we have in our unshakeable influence toolkit, but most people spend little, if any, time taking a deep look at their habitual ways of thinking and how that impacts their leadership ability.

Some researchers, such as the Laboratory of Neuroimaging at the University of Southern California, have made some estimates as to how many thoughts the average person has in a day. These estimates suggest we have somewhere between 12,000 and 60,000 thoughts in a day. However, the study of how many thoughts we have in a day is on the frontier of our understanding of the human mind. At this time, scientists don't yet agree on what constitutes a discrete thought, let alone have a proven way to accurately count the number of thoughts running through a human mind. One thing neuroscientists do seem to agree on is that the human brain does not work like a computer, which only does computations in sequence. Our brains actually process multiple thoughts at the same time.

We are not aware of our ability to think multiple thoughts at one time because many of our simultaneous thoughts are subconscious.

Given that there are 86,400 seconds in a day and that our minds process multiple thoughts simultaneously, we may actually have far more than 60,000 thoughts in a day. With all those thoughts directed intelligently – i.e. if we chose to only have positive and empowering thoughts – we could be incredibly hyper-achieving individuals. But here's the thing: it is also estimated that 60-80% of our thoughts are negative, and as much as 95% of our thoughts are repetitive.

That means, given what we know so far about the thought patterns of the human mind, the average person has somewhere between 7,200 and 48,000 negative thoughts a day – and possibly a whole lot more. And the vast majority of those negative thoughts are likely the same negative thoughts repeated again and again. Moreover, these patterns of thought – negative thought – have typically been habituated in us for so long that the neural pathways are deeply ingrained in our brains by the time we reach adulthood. Thus, as strange as it may sound, habitually negative thoughts can actually feel comforting to us. Remember our comfort zone from Chapter 2? By definition, thoughts, feelings, and behaviors that feel comfortable are deeply ingrained in our minds.

Further, it is these habitual and subconscious thought patterns that create the overarching environment that our conscious thoughts exist in. Put another way, when our automatic and unconscious thoughts are skewed negatively, our conscious, higher-order thinking is also skewed negatively – **only we don't realize how negative we are**.

In the leadership race of the 21st century, everyone is looking for a competitive edge. While the conscious and unconscious thought patterns that constitute our Mindset are deeply ingrained habits, like all habits they can be changed. Our unconscious thought patterns feel so automatic that it may seem like a tall order to change them, but to pull ahead of the competition in today's racetrack-like world, it is imperative that we consciously optimize our Mindset to become unshakeable in our influence.

WE HAVE ALL THE POWER WE NEED TO BECOME THE UNSHAKEABLE LEADER WE WANT TO BE

Our reactions often feel automatic—as if we have little or no control, but we always have a choice about how we interpret events and how we react to them. This is the danger of our never-ending cycle of reactivity: reacting to a situation unconsciously and automatically – sometimes with dire consequences.

In motorcycle racing, life itself depends not only on quick reactions but also on executing the **right** reaction quickly. For example, in the heat of battle on the racetrack, it's not uncommon for the motorcycle to slide unexpectedly. When the motorcycle begins to slide, the bike is no longer going where you want it to go. It is now likely heading off the racetrack and perhaps into a concrete wall that can do serious damage to you and your bike. Reaction time is critical, but it has to be the right reaction.

A less experienced racer's instincts will tell them to do the wrong thing in this situation. Less experienced racers will try to turn the bike even harder because the bike did not respond as expected and is now heading for a concrete wall. That split-second, automatic decision to turn harder will likely cause the previously sliding bike to immediately crash. That is because the decision to turn harder puts even more traction demands on tires that have already exceeded their traction limits.

A more experienced racer knows this and has trained himself to automatically react differently. The experienced racer reacts by turning the bike less, not more. This seems counter-intuitive because it momentarily points the motorcycle even more off track, but by temporarily taking some of the traction demands off the tires, the tires regain traction. Now, with the bike under control again, the experienced racer turns the motorcycle in the direction he needs it to go. The racer avoids hitting the concrete wall, avoids crashing altogether, and probably only loses a fraction of a second on his lap time.

Bringing this back to leadership, some leaders have lives at stake with their decisions and some don't. Either way, our leadership reactions are critical to our success in maximizing our leadership influence. Consider the saying, "It takes years to build trust and only seconds to destroy it." As a common example, some leaders struggle to keep their anger under control. With just one angry outburst at an employee, years worth of trust can be seriously undermined. Additionally, just one angry outburst at a key client can cost the organization millions of dollars in lost revenue.

One of the executives I have coached 1:1 struggled with this very issue. He was a co-founder and CEO of a technology company in Silicon Valley. He came from a military leadership background and was super smart, quick on his feet, cared about his people, and could be very inspirational. He had many good things going for him, yet he had a short fuse and would sometimes lash out when angered. His angry outbursts had already been the primary cause of a key executive leaving the company. When I first started working with him, he had serious doubts about his ability to keep his anger in check. He had a competitive streak, so I figured he'd relate well to a racing analogy. By using this racing story I've shared here, he gained a clearer understanding of how important it is to learn to override automatic reactions. Over time, by evaluating the internal stories he was telling himself and working on his emotional intelligence, he learned to override his default reaction to anger. He learned to use his anger as motivation and fuel; instead of acting it out, he now takes responsibility for his anger and channels it into positive action.

As was the case with this executive, our unconscious reactivity is based on stories that we tell ourselves about who we are, who we are not, and how the world works. By adulthood, we've typically repeated these same stories so many times that they have become largely automatic and subconscious. (Remember: 95% of our thoughts are repetitive.) The thing is: our way of viewing ourselves and the world was largely given to us by our parents (or other primary caregivers) through emotional attunement when we were young.

As children, we connect with and emotionally attune to our parents, and through that deep connection we absorb much of their belief systems. We also have a lot of direct experiences in our childhood that teach us lessons about how to think about the world and how to think about who we are in the world. Much of this attunement and conditioning happens before the age of seven.

It is only from the age of seven onward that we begin to develop the capacity to think for ourselves and decide what we believe and don't believe. Up until that point, we really have no choice but to automatically adopt our parents' beliefs about us and about the world. Our parents probably did the best they knew how to do, and many of these adopted beliefs may serve us well. But no matter how great our parents might (or might not) have been, we all have adopted some dysfunctional views of ourselves and the world, and as adults we are still being unconsciously driven by those distortions.

While our reactions often feel automatic and uncontrollable, the fact is that all of our automatic reactions were learned; therefore, they can be unlearned. We can regain control over our reactions by evaluating our Mindset and consciously choosing a more accurate and supportive Mindset – a Mindset that will enable us to more consistently be our best leadership self.

Chapter 4

Foundational Mindset Skills

JUST LIKE IN MOTORCYCLE racing where there's always another race to win, another championship to win, and a faster competitor to beat, mastering the Inner Game of Leadership is a never-ending adventure. It may be helpful to think of this chapter as Mindset 101 and the advanced Mindset skills in the following chapter as Mindset 201, or graduate level Mindset skills. Unlike a traditional undergraduate college degree and graduate degrees, however, the study of the Inner Game of Leadership is never complete.

This chapter introduces the foundational Mindset skills required for becoming unshakeable in your influence. From there, you will be well prepared to delve into the following chapter on advanced leadership Mindset skills.

How We Do Anything is How We Do Everything

Mastering our Inner Game of Leadership requires looking honestly and critically at our thoughts, feelings, and behaviors. As we take a deeper look at our Mindset and how it might be holding us back, it is important to acknowledge that how we do anything is how we do everything. What this means is that *everything* we do is an indicator of our overarching patterns of thought, feeling, and behavior.

One of the key cognitive biases that interferes when it comes to being honest with ourselves about our own limitations and flaws is what psychologists call the fundamental attribution error. In essence, the impact of this bias on our thinking is that we tend to judge other people's behavior as indicators of a character flaw and/or mal-intent, while we tend to judge our own behavior as a result of our circumstances, assuming it has nothing to do with who we are as a person or any negative intentions on our part.

The reality is that our current behavior in this moment is nearly always an indicator of our overarching pattern of thinking, feeling, and behaving; it is not just a one-off behavior that is the result of our current circumstances. To take an honest look at our Mindset, we need to accept that how we do anything is how we do everything. Only then can we take a critical enough look at ourselves in order to gain insight into our self-limiting patterns of thought, feeling, and behavior.

I didn't know it at the time, but I had a clear *how you do anything is how you do everything* moment in my first year of motorcycle road-racing. For most racers, it takes years of practice to advance up to finishing a race in the top ten. I was quite good at racing straightaway, placing as high as 5th in my first year. As a novice, it surprised me how quickly and easily racing seemed to come to me. While I was working hard at it, I loved it and wanted to win, so it often didn't feel like work.

Thus, I was, in a way, thrust into a leadership role. I became a de facto leader in motorcycle racing because of how well I was placing as a complete novice. I had no true interest in being a leader in racing, but I loved the sport and I wanted to win *really bad*. And because I was successful so quickly, a certain level of leadership was handed to me.

Many ambitious executives and leaders have a similar experience in their work. They too love what they do and they want to win – *really bad*. As a result, they may find themselves promoted into senior leadership roles before they are truly ready. They thought they were ready, but then they aren't sufficiently prepared with either their Mindset or their Heartset. Remember the Peter Principle from Chapter 2? Anyone ambitious enough will eventually be promoted to their level of incompetence, where they will begin to struggle because they have to shift their entire inner paradigm, their entire way of being. For leaders, that paradigm shift often includes letting go of being an amazing individual contributor and instead learning how to enroll, motivate, and inspire *others* to do their best work.

If you're mindful enough as you advance through the ranks, you will be able to recognize ahead of time that you need to make that inner paradigm shift if you want to continue to succeed at higher and higher levels of leadership. You will know, well before you get there, that you can't scale yourself as a leader by focusing on positional authority. You will know that you need to shift to relational authority, and you will begin to take significant steps in that direction before you get promoted too far beyond your current leadership abilities. But to do that, you have to pay attention to the signals along the way. The signals that you need to grow into a new, inner paradigm are always there, if you just listen closely enough.

In my novice year of motorcycle racing, there came a very clear signal of the inner paradigm shift that I needed to make, but I missed that signal because I was so focused on winning the top novice award – a prestigious championship award that spans all racing classes. This award is meant to highlight and feature the best of the new racers – the up-and-coming new talent in a racing organization filled with talented racers. That top novice award was a big deal to me, and I was intent on winning it.

At the mid-point of my first year of racing, I was in second place in the overall novice standings. The upcoming July race was at Sonoma Raceway, where I'd always placed my best. I was determined to move up into first place in the novice standings, and I couldn't wait to get on the track for this race!

When the start of the race finally arrived, I got a poor start, but I was able to work my way up into the top eight by the halfway point of the race. A fifth-place finish would have moved me much closer to winning that top novice award, and I was feeling really good as I could clearly envision overtaking the next few racers and moving into 5th place before the checkered flag. But with only three laps remaining in the race, I noticed a very unusual and concerning sound coming from my motorcycle. After a few corners of this disturbing sound growing worse, I realized something on my motorcycle was dragging. I then looked down and saw that one of my motorcycle's twin exhausts had started falling off the bike and was dragging on the pavement!

This was a dangerous situation because it was clear that the exhaust might soon fall all the way off and then go flying – perhaps at triple digit speeds into my motorcycle or (more likely) someone else's. The thought that immediately went through my mind was that if I didn't finish my race that day, I would certainly lose the top novice award because I would get zero points from that day's race and there would be no catching up. At the same time, some part of me knew that staying on the track with this malfunction would be risky. In motorcycle road-racing, people are injured or killed on a regular basis. If that exhaust pipe fell all the way off, the odds of injury or perhaps even death were significant. The safe, compassionate, and reasonable thing to do was for me to pull off the racetrack as soon as possible. But I didn't do that.

I stayed on the racetrack anyway – hoping I could finish the race and keep my chances of winning the top novice award alive. However, there are corner workers in every corner of the racetrack whose job it is to monitor the track for any unsafe conditions. If they notice any safety issue with a racer's motorcycle, they will give that racer what is affectionately called "the meatball flag" (a black flag with a solid orange circle in the middle); this flag indicates the racer needs to pull off the track as soon as possible because there is something unsafe about the motorcycle. It took a lap or two but, sure enough, I got the meatball flag. I was forced to pull off the racetrack, unable to complete the race, and thus scored zero points that day. I was devastated.

After the race was over, I lied. I claimed I didn't know there was anything wrong with my motorcycle until I got that meatball flag. A key mentor didn't believe me, and even in the face of skepticism from someone who was trying to help me, I stuck to my false story. Internally, I told myself that anyone in my circumstance would have done the same thing. In retrospect, being too ashamed to admit the truth was an obvious and clear signal that I didn't really believe my rationalizations. This was my own version of using the fundamental attribution error to let myself off the hook for my actions that day. Only with the writing of this book nearly twenty years later have I finally revealed the complete truth, either to myself or anyone else.

That race day when I got the meatball flag was definitely a *how you do anything is how you do everything* moment for me. The fact is: I knowingly endangered myself and others because I was overly attached to winning. I was fortunate to walk away safely that day and avoid hurting anyone else. The experience could have been a wake-up call for me, but I slept through it. Because I didn't heed the warning (or even see it as a warning at the time), I had the big 100-mph crash described in the introduction of this book a while later. I was still operating in the same way – being overly attached to winning and not caring enough about anything or anyone else.

This story is important for mastering our Inner Game of Leadership because it is quite often denial that prevents us from taking a critically honest look at ourselves. Awareness of our own limitations simply has to come before we have any opportunity to improve ourselves.

Unfortunately, in leadership there are no corner workers with meatball flags watching the work environment to ensure everyone is behaving in a reasonable and compassionate manner that maximizes our influence. In the working world, the warning signals are often more subtle than this and, therefore, even easier to deny. If we are to become unshakeable in our influence, we must be especially vigilant in our introspection and self-honesty.

Only with awareness of our Mindset limitations do we gain the opportunity to improve. Let's start by assuming that everything we do is an indicator of our overarching Mindset and not just a one-off behavior. Then, when we've done something at work or at home that we're not proud of, let's look for how that same pattern of behavior is showing up in other areas of our life.

Additionally, your answers to the following questions will help illuminate some of your Mindset blind spots:

1. Is there any part of your behavior at work that you wouldn't want your loved ones to witness?
2. If you were being completely honest with the loved ones in your life, what would you share with them now that you've never shared before?
3. What feedback have you heard from others that may have triggered you? Why did it trigger you?
4. What are the recurring patterns in your reactions at work? If you don't know, start keeping a daily log and look for the patterns.

Being overly attached to winning and our need for control are intertwined. To the mind that is overly attached to winning, what better way to ensure victory than to try to control every possibility? The possibilities in life are infinite, so we cannot possibly control everything. The mind that is overly attached to winning has a hard time accepting that fact.

LETTING GO OF CONTROL

The famous and incredibly successful race car driver Mario Andretti once said, "If everything seems under control, you're not going fast enough."

Leaders in today's always-on, racetrack-like, VUCA world simply cannot afford to try to keep everything under control. There's way too much information coming at us, too many demands on our time, and too many competing priorities. Moreover, the landscape of the world we live in is changing at such a rapid pace that we simply have to get more comfortable with less control now more than ever before. Further, as we advance into more and more leadership responsibility, we have to let go of more and more direct control over any outcomes to maximize our leadership effectiveness.

For many leaders, this is one of the scariest parts of mastering the Inner Game of Leadership. So much is at stake, *including your career*, yet we can no longer focus on directly controlling the outcomes because the span of our purview is too broad to even attempt that. One of the cruxes of being successful in senior leadership roles is being able to make this transition successfully – the transition to letting go of direct control.

As important as it is to let go of control, leaders sometimes struggle to recognize their own controlling tendencies. Here are some questions to help you identify any controlling tendencies you might have:

1. Do you have any difficulty delegating?
2. Do you struggle when others don't behave as you expect them to?
3. When you do delegate, do you give people guardrails and high-level guidance, and then truly let them run with it?
4. How willing are you to let people fail in order to allow them to learn for themselves?
5. Do you ask provocative and open-ended questions to help others find their own answers, or are you more prone to just providing answers?
6. How often do you articulate the bigger picture and strategy to others vs. the task list?
7. Do you have perfectionistic tendencies?
8. Do you have any tendencies toward micromanaging others?
9. How often do you coach and mentor others versus telling them what to do?

Letting go of control is difficult for many leaders because it is often their drive for control that has directly led them to the successes they've experienced to date. Given how hard it can be, how do we do it? From a Mindset perspective, a key consideration is how we tend to attach our self-worth as a person to external success.

The truth is: we are already in the winner's circle just by being born. The fact that we're here at all makes us perfectly worthy. Our self-worth is not defined by career success, possessions, the right family, our kids' successes, our subordinates' successes, or having the "right" education or living in the "right" neighborhood. Our need for control stems from an inner fear that not having one or more of the above "go right" means that our value as a person is threatened in some way. That fear is running our behavior as strongly as it is because we define our self-worth on attaining these external successes. The reality is that self-worth is an *inside* game not an outside game.

Until we change that inner fear, learn how to welcome more uncertainty into our lives and, thereby, learn how to function well in a world full of uncertainty, no amount of techniques for becoming less controlling are likely to help much. In short, any controlling tendencies we may have are very unlikely to change in sustainable ways unless we change the underlying beliefs driving those behaviors.

I've observed two realizations that consistently help leaders overcome the Mindset aspect of an overly strong need for control. First, recognize that no one responds optimally to their boss trying to control them – it's one of the strongest factors contributing to burnout and employees quitting their companies. Second, recognize that once we advance far enough as a leader, we cannot sufficiently scale ourselves as leaders if we're focused more on control than on influence. Even with just a dozen people working under you (either directly or indirectly), control is simply no longer scalable. *Influence is scalable.* We limit our effectiveness and the effectiveness of our organization when we allow ourselves to stay stuck in any overly controlling tendencies.

Finally, one of the most powerful techniques for letting go of our need for control is meditation. As we will see in this next section, meditation also has many other foundational benefits to our Mindset and lays important groundwork for our more advanced Mindset skills.

MEDITATION

In early 2014, Arianna Huffington said on stage at the Wisdom 2.0 conference, "2013 was the year that CEOs came out, not as gay, but as meditators."

Many business leaders have struggled to see the practical applications of meditation; it is often perceived as time-consuming, difficult, and overly passive. Some of the executives I work with will initially resist meditation as a helpful leadership Mindset tool. The most common rationale is that they don't have time for it. My answer is always the same: in today's fast-paced and always-on world, we don't have time *not* to meditate.

With meditation, we tend to get our time back, many times over, in the form of such things as:

- Reduced stress
- Less reactivity
- Increased clarity of thought
- More focus
- More creative and strategic thinking
- Better ability to communicate with empathy and compassion

All these benefits are keys to scaling ourselves as leaders through developing unshakeable influence. Putting it simply, it's more costly to allow our brain to go untrained than it is to give our brain the workout it needs by meditating.

In today's workplace, if we don't practice meditation in some form, we are likely to be out of balance in a critical way. To make that point clearer, let's look at autonomic nervous system 101.

In simple terms, our autonomic nervous system has two main subsystems: the sympathetic and the parasympathetic. The sympathetic nervous system is responsible for the fight-or-flight response that helps us overcome perceived threats to our safety by increasing our heart rate, contracting our muscles, and directing more blood flow to our muscles for fast action and strength and less to longer-term functions such as digestion and immunity. In the fight-or-flight response, the body also releases adrenaline and cortisol to give us more energy and strength in response to a physical threat.

The parasympathetic nervous system is responsible for rest, recovery, flexibility, and the feeling of being in the flow of life. This response causes our muscles to relax and our breathing and heart rates to slow; it directs more blood flow to longer term concerns of the body such as digestion and our immune system.

Both systems are important for us to survive and thrive in life. Without the sympathetic response, we'd be much less likely to survive physical threats. Without the parasympathetic response, we'd be more prone to getting sick; our bodies and minds would struggle to recover from strenuous activity, and we would have more trouble digesting foods properly.

The sympathetic response is also associated with being in action mode, being hyper-efficient task masters, and excelling at pure individual achievement. But in this response, we also have more difficulty relating to others. We tend to get tunnel vision and have more challenges seeing multiple options to solve a problem, and we struggle to think creatively and work optimally with others.

The parasympathetic response is associated with increasing our focus, becoming more open-minded and empathic, thinking more strategically, increasing our mind's ability to learn and integrate learning, better understanding others' points of view, bringing more creativity, and supporting more divergent thinking and free-flowing of ideas. The parasympathetic response strongly supports leaders in coming more often from the creative/proactive Mindset and reducing reactivity, which has been shown to drive better business results.

The sympathetic nervous system is clearly a key element that drives our never-ending cycle of reactivity. Reacting quickly and with little or no conscious thought is sometimes necessary. Split-second decisions can save lives under truly life-threatening circumstances. The problem is: in today's always-on world, our primitive amygdala often misinterprets leadership situations as threatening to our physical safety, and we end up spending far too much time in the sympathetic nervous response.

Thus, many of us live and lead from a place of imbalance between the two nervous systems. We spend too much time in the sympathetic nervous system and nowhere near enough time in the parasympathetic. This is, essentially, chronic stress.

Chronic stress is prevalent in today's world, and stress levels seem likely to accelerate further in the business world of 2021 and beyond. Chronic stress is strongly associated with heart disease, anxiety, depression, digestive problems, headaches, sleep problems, weight gain, and memory and concentration problems.

It can be a hard sell to get executives to change due to health concerns because many are overachievers and don't worry much about that seemingly far-off future when they might have a heart attack. Convincing themselves that it won't happen to them is a common mistake. Only when they actually have that heart attack will many begin to heed the warning. And, of course, by that time, a lot of irreversible damage has already been done. But here's the thing: chronic stress also **seriously impairs** our abilities as leaders in today's world because it is a key ingredient in our never-ending cycle of reactivity.

To sustainably change our thought patterns and let go of our never-ending cycle of reactivity so we can be our best leadership selves, we must first take our mind to the gym. We need a mental workout tool that develops our brains in very specific ways. We need to train our brains to increase our executive function and our capacity for understanding and relating to others while decreasing our amygdala's reactive influence on us. Think of meditation as a workout for the brain because that is exactly what it is. The results of recent research into the effects of meditation on the brain are (at least to me as a coaching geek) astonishing and heart-warming. Let's take a quick tour of one of these studies.

A recent study shows:

- In only eight weeks of meditation practice, the amygdala shrinks in size.
- The pre-frontal cortex (which is the source of/responsible for higher-order brain functions) becomes thicker.
- The "functional connectivity" between these regions, meaning how often they are activated together, also changes; the connection between the amygdala and the rest of the brain gets weaker while the connections between areas associated with attention and concentration get stronger.
- The left hippocampus (associated with learning, cognition, memory, and emotional regulation) grows thicker.
- The temporoparietal junction, associated with perspective taking, empathy and compassion, also grows thicker.
- The scale of these changes increases the more one meditates.

Put simply, as we train our brains through meditation, these results show:

- Our primal responses to stress are increasingly superseded by thoughtful ones.
- We develop an increased ability to learn and remember.
- We increase our ability to understand others' perspectives.
- We increase our capacity for empathy and compassion for others.

These are all critical developments of our brain to better position us for the relational and mindful leadership that is so clearly called for in the 21st century. Remember: 2013 was the year CEOs came out of the closet as meditators. If we're not meditating already, we're falling behind in the leadership race. If we are already meditating, going deeper into our practice will take us even further ahead of our leadership competition.

Just like athletes, leaders don't work out just for the sake of working out. We work out our brains so we can excel even more at leadership. Meditation lays the foundation for more advanced Mindset skills which require deeper concentration faculties, more self-awareness, more compassion and relationship focus, and a better ability to avoid reactivity and thereby stay more consistently in a creative/proactive Mindset.

At a broad level, there are two different types of meditation. One is passive, and the other is active. Think of passive meditation as sitting quietly, eyes closed, focused on a mantra (perhaps our breathing). On the other hand, active meditation is referred to as doing something active while meditating. One example of active meditation is walking meditation: paying close attention and being present to each and every microsecond of a walk. Another great example of active meditation is yoga. In the United States, yoga is, unfortunately, too often taught as mainly a physical discipline, but it's actually more intended to be a deep meditation that happens to also utilize the body.

The seemingly passive nature of meditation is one of the key reasons busy people who have not experienced the overarching positive benefits of meditation resist it. Executives often view it as something that might make you feel good while you're doing it, but then you have to get back to your "real life" and nothing has changed. The fact is: a consistent meditation practice will change our real lives, too. But even very experienced meditators sometimes struggle to see and experience the benefits of meditation in daily life.

That's a key reason why, in my work with leaders, I use active meditation in a very different way than is typically talked about. The active meditation we teach our clients consists of cultivating the ability to be in a quasi-meditative state in which the observer mind (the part of us that dispassionately observes our self in action) is activated **nearly all the time**. From that highly aware inner state, we are more able to consciously and mindfully choose our next step, moment by moment, every minute of every day. That may sound difficult, perhaps even impossible. I assure you that it's not.

Anyone can cultivate this ability, and the payoff is tremendous. As I mentioned before, it's a beautiful thing to witness when clients begin to master their reactivity and are able to respond to their circumstances from a more conscious, creative, and effective place. From that place, they experience a higher level of inner calm, groundedness, and confidence. Meditation is very key to cultivating and maximizing our Inner Game of Leadership.

The mental workout of meditation is a foundational skill needed for the more advanced Mindset and Heartset skills that will be detailed in subsequent chapters:

- Maximizing our Mindset
- Maximizing our Heartset
- Consciously choosing how we show up moment by moment
- Consciously taking a leadership stance every minute of every day
- Developing and deepening our emotional intelligence
- Not allowing ourselves to be run by our emotions but, instead, cultivating and using our emotions to increase our influence
- Changing our habitually negative patterns of thought that are holding us back
- Letting go of our never-ending cycle of reactivity
- Choosing a Mindset of empowerment instead of victimhood

It is beyond the scope of this book to teach you how to meditate. Many wonderful teachers, books, classes, tools, and guided meditations are widely available.

Here are some resources that I know work well:

- If you're new to meditation, start with guided meditation, like one of the many mindfulness smartphone apps
- Online, guided meditation done live with others; for example, Spirit Rock Monday night meditation is available online
- Look for local meditation classes in your area

- Meditation retreats
- Yoga classes
- Bikram (a.k.a. hot) yoga if you like more intense workouts
- NuCalm is a meditation technology that works very well to induce the parasympathetic response in an almost automatic way

Additionally, two of the common questions my clients ask are how often they should meditate and for how long. Many leaders I work with end up settling in on about 15-20 minutes per day. As a rule of thumb for beginners, I recommend a minimum practice of five minutes each day.

GRATITUDE

As renowned psychologist Rick Hanson likes to say, "The mind is like Velcro for negative experiences and Teflon for positive ones." We are wired with a negativity bias in our brains. This is, once again, related to our need for survival. If we remember vividly how we narrowly escaped the tiger that almost killed us, we have a much better chance of surviving the next time we encounter a tiger. If we remember vividly how much we enjoy watching the sunset, that doesn't directly impact our survival, so we won't remember it as strongly. But it certainly impacts our happiness level which, as we've already shown, tends to create better productivity, effectiveness, and overall outcomes in leadership.

In true survival situations, our negativity bias serves us well. But for the vast majority of leaders reading this book, we are rarely, if ever, faced with a true survival situation. However, our amygdala interprets many scenarios each day as posing some level of threat and triggers the fight-or-flight response discussed earlier.

A lot of studies have been done regarding what it takes to consciously counteract our negativity biases interpersonally. There have also been a number of studies of organizational cultures to determine the optimal level of emotionally positive experiences to emotionally negative ones in order to create the highest functioning culture. Studies support a positive:negative ratio of at least 3:1, and some studies support as much as 11:1 before it turns too Pollyanna-ish and undermines results.

I work with a wide variety of leaders, teams, and cultures and have found that many of them have a positive:negative ratio of 1:1 or less. This is abysmal, yet unfortunately it is all too common. I've also seen how changing this one aspect of culture goes a long way in creating environments with more transparency and candor, more productive conflict, better morale, and better productivity. What I recommend is to strive for at least a 5:1 ratio of positive:negative interactions.

From an individual Mindset perspective, gratitude is one of the most effective tools at overcoming our negativity bias. The fact is: everything in life, even the most seemingly negative experiences, also have a positive side. When we overly focus on the negative (which our brains will do by default), we hold ourselves and our organizations back.

One of the most helpful resources I've found for learning how to shift our Mindset to being more positive through practicing gratitude is a book called *Gratitude Works* by Robert A. Emmons. According to his research, "Gratitude has one of the strongest links to mental health and satisfaction with life of any personality trait – more so than even optimism, hope, or compassion." He goes on to say, "People are 25 percent happier if they keep gratitude journals, sleep one-half hour more per evening, and exercise 33 percent more each week."

A mind that tends to focus on the negative will tend to create more negative outcomes. Conversely, a mind that focuses on the positive will tend to create more positive outcomes. Further, due to our tendency as a species to mirror the emotions of those around us, our happiness as a leader will tend to create more happiness around us in an upward spiral fashion.

We can only get our minds to focus on the positive consistently by doing specific workout exercises for our brain. Left to its own devices, our brain will very likely turn unduly negative and undermine our leadership resilience, influence, and overall effectiveness.

The concept of a gratitude practice may sound daunting, but it's actually pretty straightforward. Here are some key tips about gratitude journaling from Robert Emmons' research:

- Gratitude journaling just twice a week is more effective than journaling more often.
- Just 5 to 10 minutes of journaling at a time is enough.
- It's important to write it down and not just think about it.
- Err on the side of writing deeply about a few things you're grateful for rather than going shallow on a lot of things you're grateful for.
- Gratitude journaling is more effective when you still remember sorrows and painful experiences, including the sense of having failed at something.
- Remember that there are always positive aspects to every single thing that happens in life.
- Be specific and detailed.
- Always look for new things to be grateful for and don't just repeat the same things.

A gratitude practice is not about being Pollyanna-ish or forgetting the things in life we've experienced as negative. On the contrary, we need negative things in life to appreciate the positive things in life. Without that contrast, we'd simply have no idea what to be grateful for because everything would feel the same. That in and of itself is one way to find the positive in something negative – we would not know how to appreciate the positive without the negative.

Further, remember that we're not being overly positive by practicing gratitude. We're simply consciously counteracting the negativity bias we all carry so that we can perform optimally. As we formally practice gratitude in this way, we will begin to notice our minds naturally turning more optimistic and grateful throughout our day-to-day activities and not just as we're journaling.

Gratitude is one of the foundational tools of Mindset. It's a very powerful tool. As just one example, I've seen some leaders go from being mediocre public speakers to becoming relaxed, poised, and powerful public speakers by using gratitude as their primary tool for overcoming stage fright.

Actor and producer Michael J. Fox said, "So much to savor, so much to be grateful for. And since I'm not sure of the address to which to send my gratitude, I put it out there in everything I do."

That's what we're striving for with our gratitude practice: to infuse gratitude into each and every thing we do. In doing so, we become more unshakeable in our influence.

Chapter 5

Advanced Mindset Skills

HAVING SPENT SOME TIME on our core foundational Mindset skills, we're now ready to delve more deeply into our Mindset work with advanced Mindset skills. All the skills highlighted in Chapter 4 are critical Mindset skills. All fuel the development of our Inner Game of Leadership and enable us to better influence ourselves and others.

Meditation is a foundational Mindset workout regimen for focusing our mind where we want. It improves our mind's ability to respond consciously, rather than react unconsciously, and activates the observer part of us that can dispassionately watch ourselves as we go about our day. Thus, our passive (or traditional) meditation practice has significant leadership benefits in and of itself. Traditional meditation also lays the groundwork in our brain to support a more active meditation practice that enables us to become fully unshakeable in our influence.

Many of the skills outlined in this advanced Mindset chapter (and much of this book) require us to practice active meditation. Active meditation is where, moment by moment, we are compassionately observing ourselves and noticing the old thought, feeling, and behavior patterns surface, then consciously making a different choice of how to show up in this moment. Over time, our new conscious choices of how to think, feel, and behave will become burned into our mind. Through this ongoing practice of active meditation, we create new automatic habits, and the old, reactive patterns of thought, feeling, and behavior will have less and less control over us.

SELF-TALK

The soap company, Dove, created an online video commercial some years ago. It opens with two beautiful women sitting at a café. One is saying to the other: "You've a big chest and really short legs. Actually, some women can make that work, but you, you've just no charm; you're just fat and ordinary."

Then the commercial reveals that some other women had earlier been asked to keep a journal of all of their thoughts. These women were then invited to come to a café for a cup of coffee where (unknown to them) two actresses are sitting at a nearby table, saying those very thoughts they'd journaled out loud to each other. "Sit up straight; otherwise your belly looks big," one says to the other. "Don't you feel horrible right now? With those large thighs and your horse's hips?" another asks.

As the women witness their own internal dialog inflicted on someone else, they are horrified by what they hear. It's a poignant scene that tells a touching story about how pervasive and pernicious our negative self-talk is and how easily we recognize the distortion and cruelty in our self-talk when it is said out loud to someone else.

While the video focuses on women's body image issues, the fact is that we all have things that we repeatedly beat ourselves up for. Remember: about 80% of our thoughts are negative and about 95% are repetitive, and we've been repeating many of those thoughts for so long that they are unconscious. Thus, while automatically beating ourselves up in ways we'd probably never say to anyone else, we struggle to recognize just how distorted and cruel our internal dialog is. Somehow, saying it aloud to someone else makes it more apparent and helps us snap out of it.

In my work with executives and leaders, I get to see firsthand just how pervasive and damaging negative self-talk is. Nearly every leader I've worked with is too often their own worst enemy. For instance, I can't recall a leader I've worked with that hasn't struggled with the imposter syndrome.

This syndrome stems from a core negative belief that we're not good enough. It often shows up in leaders with symptoms like over-preparing for presentations, fearing they will be "found out" and exposed as someone who doesn't deserve to be in their position, and constant worrying that they will let others down. When caught up in this syndrome, leaders tend to have automatic negative thoughts like, "I don't deserve to be in this role," or "I will be exposed as a fraud any day now," or "I'm not as good at my job as I should be."

The questions that I like to ask my clients are: What if you treated yourself like your own best friend? What if you only spoke to yourself in the same way that you would speak to your best friend when you're championing them to be their best selves? How much of a difference would that make in your life? The answer to that last question, almost invariably, is a **huge** difference.

Building on this, one simple technique that I have seen work well to combat our habitually negative thoughts is to take some time to do the following:

- Become aware of our automatically negative thoughts by using active meditation to dispassionately notice our automatic thoughts.
  - With the clear mind that stems from meditation practice, we can more easily regain awareness of our unconscious thoughts.
  - Once you start to get back in touch with those negative thoughts, write them down.
- With this list of some of your habitual negative thoughts, put two columns on a piece of paper.
  - Label the left column "automatic negative thoughts."

- Label the right column "best friend thoughts."
- Now, list your automatic negative thoughts in the left column.
- For each negative thought, ask yourself, "What would I say to my best friend in response to this? Write your response down in the right-hand column.

Once you have created this list, proactively re-read the best friend column to yourself. I suggest reading it to yourself every morning and every evening at a minimum. Also, throughout your day, practice active meditation to catch yourself in the act of saying your automatic negative thought, then consciously substitute your best friend column instead. This practice is simple and works very effectively if you do it consistently.

There's an entire area of psychology dedicated to this practice. It is called *Cognitive Behavioral Therapy*. It was popularized by David D. Burns in his book, *Feeling Good: The New Mood Therapy*. In that book, he presents some powerful tools for shifting our internal dialog. The approach that I use with my clients is more akin to mindfulness-based cognitive therapy. This is essentially a combination of mindfulness training (meditation) with cognitive behavioral therapy. The process of changing our automatic negative thoughts takes time. Take it one step at a time, and recognize that your work on your self-talk is likely to progress in a 'two steps forward, one step back' kind of fashion.

I assure you that the more you do the work of improving your self-talk, the more you will become unshakeable in your leadership and in your life. We can all re-wire our neural pathways no matter what our age or experience level. In fact, with diligent and mindful practice, we will see tangible benefits relatively quickly. And the more we do it, the easier it gets. Practice consciously choosing our internal dialog long enough, and eventually we reach a tipping point where we can often choose our internal dialog with relative ease. From there, our emotional and psychological well-being will be multiplied, and we will no longer allow ourselves to fall into any mental rut for long.

SELF-COMPASSION VS. SELF-ESTEEM

Self-compassion is the practice of treating ourselves well at all times, not just when we're performing well. Self-compassion is speaking kindly to ourselves, recognizing our common humanity, and the practice of being fully present to what is actually happening in our lives – moment by moment. It's about recognizing and welcoming the fact that we are imperfect human beings who sometimes make mistakes, sometimes don't do well, and sometimes struggle in all kinds of ways. In fact, part of the practice of self-compassion is recognizing that the struggle itself is a part of what we share with all of humanity. Struggle is one of the things that defines our commonality as a species.

Self-compassion is also about letting go of comparison to others as a key metric of our value as a person. As soon as we compare ourselves to others, we are more likely to turn to external validation for our self-worth, thereby putting ourselves back on the roller coaster of reactivity. At the same time, comparing ourselves against others is a constant in life. For example, comparison is the very definition of racing a motorcycle because without competitors to compare ourselves against there simply wouldn't be a race. It's when we beat ourselves up for comparing poorly, or prop ourselves up for comparing well, that we begin to base our self-worth as a human on how we compare and thereby deepen and perpetuate our never-ending cycles of reactivity.

I believe this is a major flaw underlying the concept of self-esteem and the self-esteem movement, at least as it has commonly been practiced. Self-esteem, as it is commonly understood, is conditional on our performance. If we score well on a test, win a motorcycle race, get that big promotion, get some great accolades from our boss, then we feel good about ourselves. And by definition, if we feel good about ourselves when those things are present, we are very likely to feel bad about ourselves when we do poorly on a test, when we crash out of our motorcycle race, when we're passed over for promotion, or when our boss criticizes our work.

Essentially, our self-esteem is formed based on perceiving ourselves as either a good person or a bad person. As a result, it is conditional on whatever we believe constitutes a "good person" and how we think we measure up to that standard on any given day. If we believe we meet that criteria today, we tend to feel better about ourselves. If we believe we don't meet that criteria today, we tend to feel worse about ourselves. Our minds tend to go in spirals – either an upward spiral of positivity or a downward spiral of negativity. Once our Mindset starts to head either toward positivity or toward negativity, it tends to build momentum in that direction, and it gets harder and harder to change it to go the other direction. This "mental attitude momentum" effect is a key contributor to our cycles of reactivity, endlessly cycling from emotional high to emotional low and back again.

When our mental and emotional state is dependent on external criteria being met, as soon as we believe we didn't perform well enough to meet a certain expectation of ourselves, our self-esteem essentially abandons us when we most need it. It is at the time of failure or disappointment in ourselves when we most need internal resources to draw from to prevent us from going down the spiral of negativity. Thus, the popular understanding of self-esteem, and the self-esteem movement itself, is a major contributor to our never-ending cycles of reactivity. As long as we continue to derive our self-worth from external circumstances and comparison to others, we will never be able to step off the reactivity roller coaster. A key to letting go of our never-ending cycle of reactivity is to shift our focus to internal validation rather than external validation, and an important component of validating ourselves internally is self-compassion.

What people tend to assume when imagining being more self-compassionate is fascinating. Many of us assume we need to beat ourselves up to avoid being lazy and complacent. We fear that if we let up on ourselves, we will slack off and do far less or maybe even do nothing at all. Dr. Kristin Neff, associate professor at the University of Texas, has pioneered academic research on self-compassion. The results of her research strongly suggest that the practice of self-compassion actually leads to:

- Greater motivation
- More productivity
- More creativity
- More happiness
- More life satisfaction
- More resilience in the face of adversity
- Increased capacity for compassion for others
- Less procrastination
- Less perfectionism
- Less depression
- Less anxiety
- Less controlling behavior
- Less stress

In short, self-compassion provides the benefits of self-esteem without the pitfalls of self-esteem. Further, it gives us key tools for best supporting ourselves at all times, especially when we need it most – at a time of disappointment or perceived failure. Further, greater resilience and reduced reactivity stem from the practice of self-compassion, whereas self-esteem contributes to fragility and is a key perpetuator of the cycle of reactivity, which greatly undermines our ability to thrive in today's VUCA world.

The skills we need to focus on to grow our capacity for self-compassion are:

- Meditation and mindfulness
- Improving our self-talk to be more positive and compassionate toward ourselves
- Gratitude
- Practicing a growth Mindset, where we view everything in life as learning

- Choosing to come from a Mindset of service to others
- Practicing forgiveness of ourselves and others

RECOVERING BACK TO YOUR BEST LEADERSHIP SELF WHEN THINGS GO AWRY

Things will sometimes go wrong, perhaps even really wrong. Leadership is not about avoiding the possibility of things going wrong. Leadership is about taking calculated risks to grow ourselves and take our organization to new levels while building the internal muscle of quickly getting ourselves back on track when things do go awry.

When we make a mistake, how do we treat ourselves? Do we beat ourselves up with our internal dialog? For many of us in the wake of a mistake, our internal dialog turns extremely negative. The negative way we tend to speak to ourselves only makes it harder for us to recover.

In working toward changing our attitude about failure, it's helpful to turn to other disciplines such as improvisational acting. One of the key tenets of improvisational acting is to celebrate failure. In doing so, over time the mental and emotional stigma associated with failure falls away. If you ever have the pleasure of watching highly skilled improvisational actors, you will not likely see any evidence that they ever failed on stage, yet they're often failing more frequently than you realize. The difference is: they have trained their minds to make failure a fun thing; thus, they don't get mentally stuck on it. In fact, they will often build on that "failure" in an entertaining way. As a result, the audience rarely recognizes any failures in the performance.

As we touched on in Chapter 2, the sense of failure is made up. It's a mental state, not an outcome. While we, our team, or our company may have failed to meet our current objectives, that failure was simply a necessary part of our learning. If we accept the failure for what it is – an opportunity to learn and grow on our way to success – then we will recover our best leadership self quickly. It's when we take ourselves out by stigmatizing failure and beating ourselves up that we turn a temporary circumstance we can learn from into a much longer state that we and/or our team stay stuck in.

For example, in Silicon Valley, the start-up mantra of failing fast so you can quickly learn from that failure and iteratively hone until you succeed with your new product idea is well-known. The same concept applies to growing ourselves as leaders. Fail fast; don't judge yourself; learn from your mistakes; and iteratively and relentlessly hone yourself to be the best leader you can be.

EMPOWERMENT PARADIGM VS. DRAMA PARADIGM

One of the more powerful Mindset tools I use with leaders is the Empowerment Paradigm vs. the Drama Paradigm. The Drama Paradigm is based on the Drama Triangle, originally conceived of by psychiatrist Dr. Stephen Karpman. The Empowerment Paradigm is also based on Dr. Karpman's work and on the work of authors such as David Emerald and Lynne Forrest.

Both paradigms are paradigms of thought and belief. The Drama Paradigm perpetuates drama and keeps us stuck. The Empowerment Paradigm perpetuates personal empowerment and sets us free. Understanding these two models, the ramifications of each of them, and learning how to navigate them, are key to letting go of the never-ending cycle of reactivity.

As with many of these advanced Mindset skills, the key, of course, is to recognize when you're operating from the Drama Paradigm and then consciously and compassionately shift your Mindset to the Empowerment Paradigm. But first, let's highlight what each of these paradigms means.

The Drama Paradigm is a set of beliefs that makes sense of the world in a dysfunctional and disempowering way. People living on this mental model believe in a world where there are only victims, persecutors/villains, and rescuers/heroes (see figure 5.1). It is a belief system that says some people are inherently good, some people are inherently evil, and some people need rescuing. In this mental paradigm, we can only play one of these three roles – victim, persecutor/villain or rescuer/hero – and all three roles stem from the same victimhood Mindset.

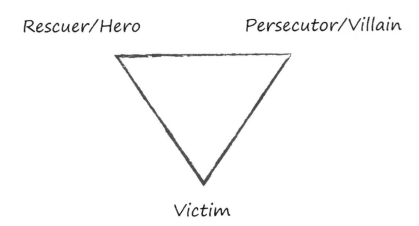

Figure 5.1 – The Drama Paradigm

This belief system is one of co-dependency and is common for those who grew up in families where addiction was present. Even without addiction, co-dependency is quite common in many family dynamics. And, remember: much of how we're showing up today as a leader is the result of our family environment. We are typically still operating under that same unconscious paradigm until we do the inner work of letting it go.

American writer and university professor David Foster Wallace tells a story of two young fish swimming together and passing by an older fish headed the other way. The older fish nods at them as he passes by and says, "Morning, boys, how's the water?" The two young fish swim on awhile and after a time one fish looks over at the other and asks, "What the hell is water?"

My experience is that the vast majority of people live primarily in the Drama Paradigm, but they're like those younger fish who cannot see the water because they've never known anything else. If any part of you is resisting how prevalent this Drama Paradigm is or perhaps thinking that this doesn't apply to you, it may be because you are one of those fish and you cannot yet see the water you're operating in.

The Empowerment Paradigm is also a triangle, but it's a triangle of – you guessed it – empowerment. In this mental paradigm, there are also only three roles. However, instead of a rescuer/hero, we have a mentor/coach; instead of a persecutor/villain, we have a challenger/ champion; and instead of a victim, we have a co-creator. This Empowerment Paradigm is a mental model that focuses on personal responsibility, respect for all, non-judgment, and empowering everyone to help themselves. Figure 5.2 shows the Empowerment Paradigm.

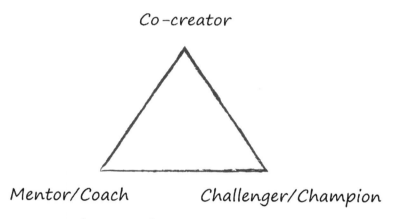

Figure 5.2 – The Empowerment Paradigm

One way to think about the differences between these two mental models is to think of the classic saying that we can either give a person a fish (rescue them) or we can teach them how to fish (mentor/coach them on how to help themselves). In order to play the role of rescuer, the rescuer needs to believe that they are somehow superior to the person they're rescuing. Put another way, we cannot rescue someone unless we believe that person cannot help themselves.

There are times when rescuing someone is called for. Think of a person drowning and a lifeguard coming to help. That lifeguard would not be very effective if he/she swam out to the drowning person and started teaching them how to swim without first rescuing them from the immediate threat to their life. On the other hand, rescuing that person to get them out of immediate danger and then teaching them how to swim so they can avoid that danger in the future is what a mentor/coach would do. A rescuer/hero who is stuck in the drama triangle wouldn't bother to teach that person how to swim. Further, the drowning swimmer stuck in the drama paradigm wouldn't feel capable of learning how to swim.

Returning to the business leadership world, consider these key questions:

- How often do we take over someone else's work because they're not doing a good enough job?
- Are we teaching people to fish by delegating, mentoring, and coaching, or are we rescuing them by directly instructing them on what to do or maybe even doing it for them?

As in the case of the drowning swimmer, there might be times in business leadership when there is an immediate need to rescue. Perhaps there's an upcoming presentation to your board and your subordinate presents you with a slide deck that is sub-par. There's too little time before the board meeting to coach them through it, so you fix it yourself. That is likely justified, as long as you circle back soon after the board meeting and mentor that subordinate so they get the learning they need to up their game. In my experience, too many leaders will avoid the mentoring afterward, and in doing so they perpetuate the need to rescue that subordinate. If we struggle to delegate, mentor, and coach others to develop and grow, we are likely in the habit of rescuing.

As another example of how important it can be to shift off the Drama Paradigm and onto the Empowerment Paradigm, a senior director I coached went from being at serious risk of being laid off to securing a role reporting to the COO to lead high-visibility and high-impact special projects by shifting her Mindset to the Empowerment Paradigm. She was a strong performer, but the company was struggling financially and imminent lay-offs were announced. Given the depth of the lay-offs, no one was safe – not even a good performer like her. To make matters worse, the announcement came at a time when she had transitioned out of her prior role and had not yet been placed anywhere else in the organization. She wanted to maintain her employment, but given the precariousness of her situation, she was in a victim Mindset. She was trying to just lay low and wait and see what happened.

As her coach, I knew that approach was not likely to serve her well. It's times like this that it is most important to take matters into our own hands and advocate for ourselves. I introduced her to the Drama Paradigm and the Empowerment Paradigm. Within a few conversations, her Mindset shifted to one of being a co-creator rather than a victim. Once her Mindset was in an empowering place, she took more responsibility for the outcome of the lay-offs and professionally and assertively advocated for herself with several key executives – landing in a great role in the end.

The key to this aspect of improving our Mindset is building two essential skills. The first skill is to self-identify when we're operating from the Drama Paradigm. The second skill is to consciously shift our Mindset from the Drama Paradigm to the Empowerment Paradigm. If we find ourselves operating from the Victim node on the Drama Paradigm, we can shift ourselves to acting as a Co-Creator on the Empowerment Paradigm. If we see ourselves operating from the persecutor/villain node, we can shift ourselves to acting as a challenger/ champion. Finally, if we find ourselves operating from the rescuer/ hero node, we can shift ourselves to acting as a coach/mentor. Figure 5.3 shows these transitions visually.

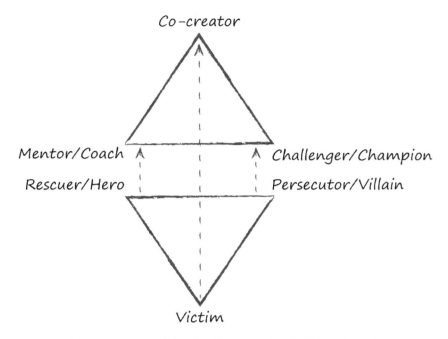

Figure 5.3 – Transitioning from Drama to Empowerment

To help you self-identify when you are operating from the Drama Paradigm and to help you shift yourself onto the Empowerment Paradigm, here are some specific tips that I know work well.

TRANSITIONING FROM VICTIM TO CO-CREATOR

When we are operating from a victim Mindset, we believe things are happening to us and that we have little or no control over what is happening. We feel unable to help ourselves out of the current challenges we're facing. A key characteristic of this Mindset is to avoid taking responsibility for ourselves. We tend to give up and want to be "saved" by someone or something else rather than taking initiative to save ourselves. This Mindset often includes perceiving ourselves as helpless, powerless, and unable to improve ourselves.

When in this Mindset, we are likely to say things to ourselves like: *It's never going to get better. Why do people always treat me this way?*

Other people will never change, so I might as well give up trying. Some trigger words to become aware of are "always" and "never." These are the words of a mind stuck in black/white thinking – a key indicator that we're operating from the Drama Paradigm.

To shift from a victim Mindset to a co-creator Mindset, we need to focus on what we **do** have control over. We need to focus on our contribution to the current challenges we're faced with. We need to take responsibility for our lives and stop waiting for anyone or anything else to "save" us. We need to look inside ourselves and ask, *What can I do to improve this situation?* We need to see ourselves as co-creators in everything we experience, and not as victims of what we experience. We need to focus on taking responsibility for our role in everything and stop blaming others. That's not to say that others aren't also responsible. It is to say that we need to focus on what we have the most control over – ourselves.

When we are coming from a co-creator Mindset, we will feel much different. We will feel empowered. We will feel connected to others, even those that might be persecuting us. We will perceive ourselves as agents of our own destiny. We will believe that we can – and should – influence nearly any situation for the better. We are proactive. We look for, and expect to find, the win-win for everyone.

In a co-creator Mindset, we are likely to be thinking things like: *I know I have a role in this situation; how can I change it for the better? This person is being difficult right now; how can I help soothe them? What do I have control and influence over in this situation?* Notice that our self-talk as a co-creator involves more questions and possibilities and that it avoids black/white thinking.

TRANSITIONING FROM RESCUER/HERO TO MENTOR/COACH

When we are operating from a rescuer/hero Mindset, we tend to believe that people need to be saved, helped, and rescued. In this Mindset, we tend to see others as more flawed than ourselves and, thus, in need of our "help." A prime example of this Mindset in action is the leader who takes over when their subordinate is struggling rather than coaching/mentoring that subordinate to step up. A key characteristic of this Mindset is to take too much responsibility for other people and not enough responsibility for ourselves.

In this Mindset, we pride ourselves on our ability to step in and be the hero. In fact, we unconsciously look for opportunities to be a hero because we've defined our self-worth as being able to rescue others. When in the Mindset of a rescuer/hero, our self-talk likely includes thoughts like: *This person needs me. I know how to do this, so I will just do it for them. This person will never be able to step up, but that's okay.*

To shift from a rescuer/hero Mindset to the Mindset of a mentor/ coach, we need to believe that all people are fully capable of helping themselves. Further, we need to believe that if we step in and save people, we're actually doing them a dis-service by pre-empting the opportunity for them to save themselves. We need to realize that our tendency to be the hero is actually detrimental to the other person's well-being.

Instead of defaulting to hero mode, we need to default to mentor/ coach mode. This means treating everyone with respect and inviting them to take more responsibility for themselves. Rescuing, or being the hero, is actually a form of enablement. By repeatedly rescuing another, we enable them to stay stuck in their own victim Mindset. Others will be better served when we, instead, expect them to take care of themselves and support them in their learning and growth by playing the role of a coach/mentor for others.

When we are operating from the Mindset of a coach/mentor, we are respecting everyone for who they are while also inviting them to become better versions of themselves. We refrain from being the hero or trying to save anyone and recognize that the only person that can save anyone is themselves. In doing so, we encourage others to step up and be more productive, more independent, and more effective.

In the Mindset of a coach/mentor, we are likely to ask ourselves questions like: *What's the most effective way for me to support this person's growth? How can I best support this person without taking over and crowding out their learning? What tools or skills does this person need to overcome this challenge, and how can I make sure they have access to those tools and have the opportunity to develop the needed skills?*

TRANSITIONING FROM PERSECUTOR/VILLAIN TO CHALLENGER/CHAMPION

When we are operating from the persecutor/villain Mindset, we believe that we need to protect ourselves from possible persecution by others. Ironically, our way of protecting ourselves from possible persecution is to persecute others. We assume that there are only winners and losers in life, and the last thing we want is to be a loser. In this Mindset, we are often overly aggressive and tend to dominate and control others to get what we want and protect ourselves from imagined potential harm.

In this mindset, we tend to think of ourselves as superior to others. We tend to blame and criticize others profusely while avoiding looking inside of ourselves or evaluating our own behavior objectively. We also tend to be suspicious of others and view them as potential threats to our well-being. In response to this fear, we try to control others and may seek to "win" at any cost. This Mindset is the one most commonly associated with bullying behavior.

The inner dialog running through our minds when we're in this Mindset is likely to include things like: *I know what's best for everyone here. I need to win this argument or we're going to go the wrong direction. They deserve to be treated this way.*

To shift from a persecutor/villain Mindset to a challenger/ champion Mindset, we need to learn to care more about other people's growth and learning than caring about protecting ourselves from potential harm. To shift out of the persecutor/villain Mindset, we look inside ourselves and objectively assess our behaviors and how they impact others. We recognize just how our highly critical nature negatively affects others and holds us back.

In the Mindset of a challenger/champion, we ease up on our harsh criticism of others. We learn to more genuinely care about others and look to support them breaking through to another level of confidence and ability. From the Mindset of a challenger/champion, we authentically try to help others by challenging them to step into being better versions of themselves. We use our ability to criticize and turn it into constructive and compassionate feedback instead of tearing people down. We can still be direct in our delivery of that feedback, but we do it with compassion and authenticity.

In the Mindset of a challenger/champion we recognize our own fears and fallibility. We learn to let go of any unconscious beliefs that people are out to "get" us. Instead, we substitute a more compassionate and realistic belief system that most people are not consciously focused on harming us in any way. We also learn to believe that nearly everyone is doing the best they know how to do given the awareness, skills, and confidence they currently have.

In the Mindset of a challenger/champion, we are likely to think: *How can I help this person to be a better version of themselves? What's the difficult truth this person needs to hear, and how can I deliver it in a way that they can hear it? How can I help create the best outcome for everyone here and not just for me?*

When it comes to the three Mindsets of the Drama Paradigm, we all have a predominant or default Mindset that we gravitate toward. Some leaders have a predominant Mindset of the victim, some have a predominant Mindset of a rescuer/hero, and some have the predominant Mindset of a persecutor/villain. To master your Inner Game of Leadership, it will be important for you to recognize which Mindset is predominant for you and then use the suggestions here to regularly shift your Mindset to the corresponding node on the Empowerment Paradigm.

It's also important to recognize that everyone has all three of the drama Mindsets in them. In different contexts we will often shift from one of these drama Mindsets to another. In fact, even in one conversation with one person we may shift between these drama

Mindsets as the conversation unfolds. What we want to focus on here is noticing when we're on the Drama Paradigm, being specific with ourselves about which Drama Mindset we've fallen into, and then consciously shift ourselves to the corresponding Mindset on the Empowerment Paradigm.

As we learn to live more and more in the Empowerment Paradigm, we will become more effective in our dealings with others. We will create less drama by being less reactive, and we will thereby experience less drama. We will also more quickly recognize when others are coming from the Drama Paradigm. We will have compassion for them while still being able to effectively model operating from the Empowerment Paradigm. In doing so, we will invite those around us to join us in this more effective and peaceful paradigm. Note that peaceful doesn't mean without conflict. It means that conflict is welcomed as a necessary part of making the best decisions, and that conflict is handled with more grace and ease because unnecessary drama is minimized.

Everything Is a Gift

As we progress in our Mindset journey, we will benefit from looking at everything in life as a gift. And I do mean everything, including the most difficult or painful experiences. We actually learn and grow the most through our painful experiences, but we have to allow ourselves to savor and learn from them while not beating ourselves up or wallowing in the pain. As we practice gratitude more and more, we will begin to see that everything in life has both a positive and a negative side. Our gratitude practice will enable our mind to increasingly see the positive in everything.

There will always be outcomes, people, and circumstances that take us by surprise, disappoint us, set us back, leave us feeling like a failure and hurt us – maybe even hurt us a lot. We have a choice when this happens. We can accept the unexpected outcome, learn from it, freely experience and release our emotions (more on that in the Heartset section) and move through it all to resolution as quickly as possible; conversely, we can resist the unexpected by wishing it were different, over-indulging in our feelings, mentally beating ourselves up, emotionally beating our team up, or otherwise going off the racetrack and into the concrete wall on the side of the track.

This is not about necessarily liking any unexpected or disappointing outcomes. This is about accepting 'what is' versus rejecting 'what is.' The more energy we spend rejecting any problems at hand, the less energy we have available to solve the problems at hand. The enemy in this case is actually our own expectations. When faced with the unexpected, we must release any expectations we had about how it was supposed to go; we must deal with the reality of what has actually happened versus what we imagined would happen.

Some questions you can ask yourself to help shift your perspective and release what you thought was going to happen are:

- What can we learn from this?
- How can we move forward?
- How can we fail quickly, with no judgment, and move to a solution focus without stepping over or missing the learning from what went wrong?

Resisting, denying, or avoiding any reality that is staring us in the face does nothing other than feed our ego and our need to be right. The longer we feed our ego in this way, the longer it will take us to solve the problem. Seeing everything as a gift helps us to quickly accept our unexpected circumstances so we can see them as clearly as possible and then move into solution mode. If we find ourselves more attached to being right than to solving the problem at hand, we're heading in the wrong direction.

Seeing everything as a gift is essentially an advanced form of gratitude practice. Some questions to help you see everything as a gift are:

- How can we be grateful for disappointment?
- How can we be grateful for failure?
- How can we be grateful for pain? For loss? For **everything**?

We can only change 'what is' when we accept and choose to be grateful for 'what is.' Including ourselves.

Chapter 6

Winning the Leadership Race with Your Mindset

I STILL REMEMBER VIVIDLY the first time I won a motorcycle road-race, while still only in my second year of racing. It was a peak achievement for sure! At the start of the race, I nearly had the "hole shot" (which in motorcycle racing means you take the lead immediately), but one of my competitors "shut the door" on me (cut me off) in the first corner, and I settled into second place. Heading into the final corner on that first lap, I knew my competitor was not as strong on the brakes into this corner, and I "out-braked" him (passed him on the brakes while entering the corner) and took the lead of a motorcycle race for the first time in my life.

It was completely exhilarating! However, leading a race for the first time can be a little eerie too. Up until then, I'd always had other racers in front of me who were setting the pace, and I was chasing them. Now, for the first time, I was the one setting the pace for the entire field of racers. My Mindset was in a really good place that day, and I was able to settle in and do my laps without any lapses in concentration. It wasn't easy though. My competitors and I were "dicing" (passing each other back and forth) throughout the race until the last lap. I was able to simply stay focused on my inner and outer work of going my fastest.

It was a very exciting race trading the lead so many times. I was up against racers with a lot more experience than me, and I actually managed to be in the lead for the majority of the race! In retrospect, it's remarkable as such a new racer that I was consistently able to pass back into the lead when I was overtaken, and because I was so present, I didn't think twice about that while it was happening. I was still in the lead when I got the white flag (signaling that this was the final lap of the race). I remember feeling pleasantly surprised to still be in the lead on the start of the final lap. Then I immediately thought, *Today is a HUGE success for me, and this is a HUGE WIN for me no matter what happens on this last lap.* And you know what? I went 0.8 seconds faster than ever before on that final lap of the race.

I can still replay the "video" in my memory as I was approaching the finish line on that final lap, watching the starter grab the checkered flag when he saw me coming up the final straight, and then throwing the checkered flag in an exuberant way as I won my first motorcycle race ever!

Motorcycle road-racing is a game of microseconds. At the top levels of the sport, it is often only a few tenths of a second per lap that separate the best racers from the rest. At that level, eight tenths of a second improvement in one lap is very significant. Further, that lap time on the final lap of my first race win (when I was the most tired and my tires were the most worn) was an all-time track record for my racing class. Even all these years later, that track lap record still stands. And since that particular track configuration at Sonoma Raceway no longer exists, I'm confident it will stand for quite some time.

I have wonderful memories of my first race victory, and I got goose bumps just now writing about it. That experience is the kind of peak performance that this book is about. It is about cultivating our inner game such that it gives us the maximum amount of time excelling – doing our very best moment by moment. And with enough of those peak moments strung together, pretty soon we've got some amazing outcomes we may have never thought possible.

What I want to focus on here is the Mindset piece of what happened for me in that race. On the final lap, my Mindset shifted, and I completely thought of myself as a winner already, regardless of the outcome. I was going quite fast before then, leading the majority of the race against more experienced racers, yet when I shifted my Mindset to think of myself as a winner "no matter what," my performance improved immediately. Perhaps I would have won the race anyway. It's impossible to know. But one of the beauties of motorsports is the immediate feedback loop, and my last lap of the race was remarkably faster than ever before.

Chapter 4 began with another story about racing in my novice year. In that story, I was so attached to (basing my self-worth on) winning, that I endangered myself and everyone else on the track while knowingly proceeding to race with a dangerous malfunction on my motorcycle. A little over a year later, I won my first race, and while I didn't fully get it yet, I began to understand the keys to maximizing performance while under pressure.

One of the keys to maximum performance in any endeavor, including leadership, is to not be overly attached to any outcome. Instead, focus on being fully present, moment by moment, doing exactly what is needed to achieve your goals. As soon as we focus too much on winning, we're a lot less likely to be able to function at our best. It feels like a paradox, and it is. There's no question that it takes tremendous focus and drive to win anything worth winning in life. There's no way I could have been in a position to win that race if I hadn't been extremely focused – driven to the point of obsession to be honest. And on that final lap, when I relaxed even more by telling myself I was already a winner no matter what, I became less attached to the outcome and went faster than ever, leaving a track record in my wake. That's the kind of performance that is possible when we maximize our Mindset using these skills.

Before closing out this Mindset section of the book, let's look again at our model of reactivity to illustrate what we're achieving as we optimize our Mindset. As we get better and better at Mindset, we will recalibrate our reactions to our circumstances to be more accurate, and we will begin to detach our sense of self-worth from our achievements. As a result, we will become calmer, more grounded, more positive, and more able to see our current circumstances as just neutral information to create from rather than react to.

In this new illustration of the model of reactivity (see figure 6.1), the gray line shows our prior level of reactivity, and the dark line shows how much less reactive we have become because of our improved Mindset. Note that the dark line suggests that we still have emotional highs and emotional lows. The difference is that they're now much more congruent with reality.

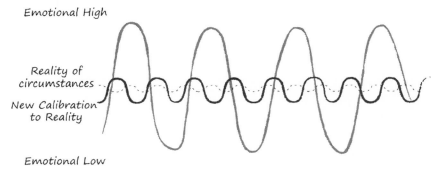

Figure 6.1 – Reactivity Model with Improved Mindset

To summarize the Mindset part of this book into just one paragraph:

Every moment of every day, **think of yourself as a winner no matter what**. Don't just think it consciously; believe it in your unconscious mind. That's exactly what you've been working on with the foundational and advanced Mindset skills. When you think of yourself as a winner no matter what, you have nothing to prove – even to yourself. From that place of having nothing to prove to anyone, you will (perhaps counter-intuitively) become even more driven to excel, more focused on your goals, more able to perform at your very best, and more able to have fun and enjoy the process every step of the way.

In the next section of the book about Heartset, you will learn how to feel this in your heart and your soul. You will also learn how to relate to others in a way that helps them feel this way about themselves, thereby taking your influence to a more unshakeable level.

PART 3

Heartset

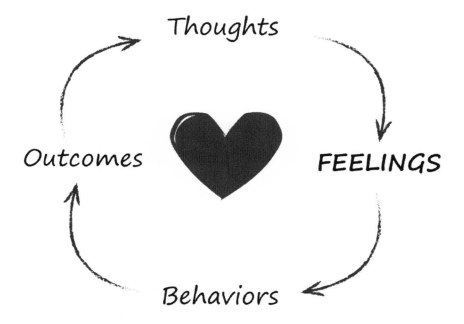

Heartset Definition:
    Our prevailing emotional tone, our ability to constructively navigate the emotions of ourselves and others, and our habitual ways of interacting and communicating with others.

Chapter 7

Introduction to Heartset

TO THE CASUAL OBSERVER, it's easy to assume that motorcycle road-racing is a completely solo sport. Part of the allure of motorsports is exactly that idea – that a single person is putting their life on the line racing a motorcycle at triple digit speeds solely for the sake of glory and the pursuit of excellence. The romanticized vision that it's just the rider and their machine against other riders and their machines in a death-defying battle to show who is the fastest is an enticing one. But it's a lie.

For every winner of any motorcycle race worth winning, there are a multitude of people behind them. For starters, while a great racer can go quite fast on a sub-par machine, they can't break the laws of physics and go faster than their motorcycle will allow. The only way to have a motorcycle that is capable of winning is to have a great team of mechanics, machinists, engine builders, suspension tuners, tire experts, engineers, manufacturers, and racing managers behind you.

Then there's the rider. The rider needs to be at their best both mentally and physically, which is only possible with great coaches, mentors, trainers, family, and friends. Finally, all these different people need to be aligned, communicating well, and working together seamlessly to have a chance at winning. So, while the "show" of motorcycle racing appears to be all about the lone racer and their machine, there's an army behind that racer, or he simply wouldn't be able to win.

The romanticized version of leadership looks and feels similar to the romanticized version of winning a motorcycle race. In today's racetrack-like world, it is the leader who knows how to inspire, motivate, and enroll people who will "win" the leadership race. But just like in motorcycle racing, great achievements require a high-functioning organization involving many people. As leaders, we must remain humbly aware of our complete dependence on others to get our job done. And because we are so completely dependent on others, we must be vigilant in optimizing our Heartset.

When it comes to influencing others to do their best work, no factor is more important than our Heartset—our prevailing emotional tone, our ability to constructively navigate the emotions of ourselves and others, and our habitual ways of interacting and communicating with others. For starters, studies suggest that 60-80 percent of our influence on others is non-verbal. Further, our non-verbal influence is based primarily on our inner state, and above all it is based on our inner emotional state. In his insightful book, *Primal Leadership*, Daniel Goleman highlights this when he writes, "Because emotions are so contagious – especially from leaders to others in the group – leader's first tasks are the emotional equivalent of good hygiene: getting their own emotions in hand." And that's not just pithy conjecture. Empirical research has shown that emotional climate alone is predictive of high profit and high growth companies versus low profit and low growth companies a whopping 75% of the time. Further, 50-70% of an employee's perceptions of the emotional climate are driven by their immediate boss.

And that's just the tip of the iceberg. In the last few decades there has been an explosion in our understanding of the impacts of emotional and relational intelligence on business results. Here are some examples:

- A study led by behavioral economist Daniel Kahneman determined that people would rather do business with someone they like and trust than someone they don't, even if that less likeable person has a better product or service.
- Another study by the Center for Creative Leadership showed that the primary causes of executive derailment include difficulty navigating change, poor interpersonal relations, and an inability to work well in teams.
- And on a personal level, another study by the Carnegie Institute of Technology demonstrated that 85% of an individual's financial success is due to skills in relational and emotional intelligence such as leadership, communication, and negotiation, and only 15% depended on technical competence.

Everything in leadership is co-created, yet people pay the closest attention to the Heartset of their most senior leaders and then tend to mimic what they witness. As a result, the emotional and relational climate of the organization has a tendency to trickle from the top down to the bottom. Thus, optimizing our Heartset is paramount when it comes to driving the best business results.

EMOTIONAL AND RELATIONAL INTELLIGENCE DRIVE THE BEST BUSINESS RESULTS

In my experience, one of the biggest challenges executive leaders face is getting access to timely, accurate, and actionable information about what is truly going on in the organization. For most organizations, by the time information has reached the executive team it has been watered down, filtered, and delayed so many times that it's almost completely useless. Thus, when an executive decision misses the mark, executives may be mystified by why it didn't work while lower-level employees often wonder, "WHAT were they thinking?" Most importantly, in any sizable organization each errant decision can easily cost millions of dollars due to costs like lost market share, lower productivity, undermined employee morale, and loss of key people who leave the organization out of frustration. In larger organizations, the cost of this cultural norm of misinformation can be hundreds of millions, or even billions, of dollars.

As leaders, we might be tempted to blame those below us for not being more honest. The truth is that leadership bears the most responsibility for any dishonesty or withholding of information. That is because by the time any employee is working in our organization they've been conditioned – probably for decades – against risking the possibility of looking ignorant, incompetent, or negative. This conditioning generally begins at a very young age and is reinforced again and again by family environments, school systems, and prior employers. Thus, whether we like it or not, we inherit this rampant conditioning with each person we hire.

For people to feel comfortable enough to risk looking bad by speaking a difficult truth, they need to believe that they are operating in a psychologically safe environment. Harvard professor Amy Edmondson, a leading expert on this topic, describes psychological safety as "a belief that one will not be punished or humiliated for speaking up with ideas, questions, concerns or mistakes." Given the decades of conditioning we're up against, to create a psychologically safe environment we leaders need to proactively, consciously, and relentlessly counteract the tendency to withhold, delay, and water down information by sharpening our emotional and relational intelligence. If we fail to do that, we will inevitably be misinformed, and it will largely be our own fault.

As a further example of how optimizing our Heartset can drive better business results, let's look at the costs of not processing and expressing anger in a relationally intelligent way. In Chapter 3 (Introduction to Mindset) we walked through an anecdote of a CEO working to increase his emotional intelligence and thereby learn to process and express his anger in a relationally intelligent way instead of being uncivil to others. Incivility (being rude, disrespectful, lashing out, or even being verbally abusive) is one of the most common dysfunctional ways in which anger is expressed in the workplace.

To better quantify the business impact of this behavior, let's take a look at the results of a detailed study that was done on incivility in the workplace. In this study, survey respondents were asked a series of questions soon after experiencing incivility. This is how they answered:

- 48% intentionally decreased their work effort
- 47% intentionally decreased time spent at work
- 38% intentionally decreased the quality of their work
- 80% lost work time worrying about the incident
- 63% lost work time avoiding the offender
- 66% said their performance declined
- 78% said their commitment to the organization declined

Clearly, the business impact of incivility in the workplace is quantifiably significant, and this is just one common Heartset challenge leaders face in today's world.

In the context of mastering our Inner Game of Leadership with our Heartset, it is also important to recognize that in the western world we have been trained to believe in the primacy of the rational mind over the emotional mind—**but recent studies have significantly undermined this foundational belief.** For example, Antonio Damasio, a professor of Neuroscience at the University of Southern California, led a study of people who had suffered such severe brain damage in the part of their brains that integrates thought and feeling that they had greatly inhibited ability to feel emotions. The study found that these people struggled to make even basic decisions about what to eat. They could rationally articulate the pros and cons of each food choice, but they struggled to actually make a decision about which food to consume.

Further, when confronted with financial investment choices, they had a tendency to choose highly risky financial investments even to the point of bankruptcy. This was because they could not connect any emotional fear of loss to their rational understanding of the investment as highly risky. And in yet another compelling study, the research suggests that emotion-based decision-making can actually be more robust than rational decision-making when it comes to volatile, uncertain, complex, and ambiguous (a.k.a. VUCA) choices – pretty much the exact kinds of choices that many leaders, teams, and organizations are faced with today.

Finally, one of the biggest reasons why Heartset is critical to mastering our Inner Game of Leadership is that people tend to do their best work when they are the most connected with themselves, with each other, and with something bigger than themselves. But the unfortunate reality is that we're suffering from a crisis of disconnection.

THE CRISIS OF DISCONNECTION

It is ironic that, in a world where technology enables us to be more connected than ever, we report feeling more disconnected than ever. In fact, reported *loneliness has more than doubled since the 1980s* – and this is not accounting for the increased loneliness many of us are feeling as I write this during the time of the COVID-19 pandemic.

Our crisis of disconnection is not limited to social connection. It is occurring at all three of the levels we crave and need to function at our best:

- Connection to ourselves
- Connection to each other
- Connection to something bigger than ourselves

Regarding connection with ourselves, we already covered in the Mindset portion of this book how much we all tend to be disconnected from ourselves in today's always-on world. Additionally, we detailed many of the business benefits of being more connected with ourselves through practices such as:

- Taking an honest, critical, and compassionate look at our thoughts, feelings, and behaviors
- Positive thinking
- Meditation
- Gratitude
- Improving our self-talk
- Self-compassion
- Cultivating inner validation versus outer validation

Regarding the crisis of disconnection with each other, more than 40% of adults today report feeling lonely. In the work environment, many employees and *half* of CEOs report feeling lonely in their roles. Additionally, we know that those who have at least one close friend at work are seven times more likely to be fully engaged and report their job satisfaction as 50% higher. We also know that those with strong social connections at work tend to produce higher quality work and are absent from work less often. But a whopping 42% report having no friends at work whatsoever.

Further, according to Vivek H. Murthy, the 19th surgeon general of the United States, "At work, loneliness reduces task performance, limits creativity, and impairs other aspects of executive function such as reasoning and decision making." Persistent loneliness also contributes to chronic stress, which, as we touched on in Chapter 4, can "hijack your brain's prefrontal cortex, which governs decision-making, planning, emotional regulation, analysis and abstract thinking." Lastly, social loneliness reduces lifespans more than drinking or obesity and as much as smoking 15 cigarettes a day!

Regarding the crisis of disconnection with something bigger than ourselves, we know that employees who derive meaning and purpose from their work (i.e. connection to something bigger than themselves) are 3x more likely to stay with their employer and are 1.4x more engaged at work. Also, according to bestselling author and University of Houston professor Brené Brown's qualitative summary of her empirical research, "When our belief that there's something greater than us, something rooted in love and compassion, breaks, we are more likely to retreat to our bunkers, to hate from afar, to tolerate bullshit and to dehumanize others."

And finally, in his New York Times best-selling book, *Drive*, Daniel H. Pink highlights a study called "the candle problem." This is a highly repeatable study that turns our understanding of business incentives on its head. Essentially, what the study shows is that our belief in money as the most effective incentive to motivate employees is fundamentally flawed. The truth is that in today's VUCA world, money as the primary incentive is more likely to undermine performance than it is to enhance it. That doesn't mean that money doesn't matter as an incentive. It means that in a VUCA world, throwing more money at an employee who is already paid fairly is more likely to undermine their performance than to improve it.

So what are the most effective motivators of people? According to Pink's meta-analysis of the research, the three key things that most motivate people to do their best work are autonomy, mastery, and purpose (connection to something bigger than ourselves).

There is clearly a crisis of disconnection in the world today, and that crisis has severe consequences in the business world. This is not an issue that any leader can afford to ignore. If our leadership and the environment we're creating is not one of connection, the environment we're leading will default to being a transactional climate where people retreat into themselves and behave in overly self-serving ways. By maximizing our leadership Heartset, we can inspire others to do their best work by fostering a deeper sense of connection on all these levels.

WE HAVE ALL THE POWER WE NEED TO BECOME UNSHAKEABLE IN OUR HEARTSET

Our prevailing emotional tone, emotional reactions, and habitual ways of interacting with others (a.k.a. our Heartset) may feel automatic and unconscious and, therefore, out of our control. But like all habits, these habits have been learned and can be unlearned. Recall from Chapter 3 in the Mindset section of this book that we have all the power we need to become the unshakeable leader we want to be. In Chapters 4 and 5, we learned Mindset techniques for unlearning our habitual thoughts and reactions and replacing them with thoughts and reactions that are more supportive of maximizing our Inner Game of Leadership. Our Heartset practice will build on our Mindset skills to extend our habit change to include optimizing our Heartset and not just our Mindset. Thus, the skills in this Heartset section are dependent on some level of mastery, or at least a smidgeon of comfort, with the Mindset skills first.

One of the Mindset skills that we will be building on here is our practice of active meditation – compassionately catching ourselves in the act of our habitual Heartset behavior and consciously replacing it with the unshakeable influence Heartset skills covered in the next two chapters. Just like with our Mindset improvement, once we've repeated our active meditation enough times, new neural pathways will begin to ingrain in our mind, and these new Heartset habits will become our new normal.

Keep in mind that our current Mindset and Heartset habits have likely been ingrained and reinforced in our minds and hearts for decades by now. Decades worth of habit reinforcement doesn't change overnight. Yet, as we've covered in detail, the payoffs to us individually and to our organizations are tremendous. If we ever start to believe that this work might be too hard, it's helpful to recognize that it is largely about returning to ourselves. Returning to the higher truth about who we are, who we are not, and our place in the world in this lifetime. When we commit ourselves to the path of mastering our Inner Game of Leadership, there simply can be no stopping us.

On the topic of returning to ourselves, I want to share two brief stories about my son, Indiana (Indy), whom I sometimes view as one of my greatest teachers.

My parents, Indy, and I have a semi-regular habit of visiting Orange County in Southern California for vacations. We all enjoy

Disneyland, the beaches, and the warmer weather in the area. The drive from our home in Northern California is about six hours, which is a lot to ask of a five-year-old boy. On this particular trip, by the time we arrived at our destination and were getting settled into our home away from home, Indy was in a bad mood; he was complaining, negative, and grouchy.

As I was about to start talking to Indy about his mood, he insisted on going outside into the fenced-in backyard alone. I honestly welcomed the chance to get a brief break from his bad mood before speaking to him about it. About six minutes later, he came back into the house in a much more jovial and fun-loving mood – as was typical for him at that age. I asked him about his mood change, and he said that he just needed some time alone. At age five, he didn't know how to (or care to) articulate it more than that, but it was remarkable. With my mouth agape in stunned silence, he then went on his merry way playing with his Lego guys.

Fast forward to the age of eight. As was our usual routine then, I had picked Indy up from school one afternoon. As we were driving home, he shared with me how a friend at school had told him that her mother had forbidden her from playing with him because he looks like an alien. I asked him how that made him feel, and he immediately said, "sad and angry." Impressed with his honest and self-aware answer, I then asked him about strategies for addressing this situation. He suggested that he could speak to the child directly about how that wasn't OK with him, and he also asked if we could call her parents. Again – I was impressed with his answer and felt no need to add anything.

My key takeaway from those two stories is that, in some ways, improving our Heartset is more about unlearning poor habits and returning to what we instinctively knew when we were young than it is about learning anything new. If a five-year-old, and then an eight- year-old child, can be this aware of his emotions, express them intelligently, and take appropriate and mindful action based on those emotions, anyone can do it.

As we transition into the next two chapters on Heartset skills, it will be helpful to keep in mind that, like our Mindset, much of our Heartset work is an internal journey, and "Everyone has a plan until they get punched in the face." Relationships involve many things and, hopefully, not getting punched in the face. This Mike Tyson quote illustrates the point that it's relatively easy to be emotionally intelligent, mindful, and grounded when we're operating in a vacuum by ourselves. It's much harder to come from our best Inner Game of Leadership while in the fluidity of relationship with others.

Relationships are dynamic, and we simply cannot optimize our Heartset skills while solely working alone. Thus, the Heartset skills detailed in the following two chapters will focus first on our inner Heartset work and then on our relational Heartset work that can only be done in relationship with others.

Chapter 8

Inner Heartset Skills

EMOTIONAL INTELLIGENCE – WHAT IS IT?

EMOTIONAL INTELLIGENCE GETS A lot of hype these days. That's great because it means that it's gaining mindshare and its importance is becoming more recognized. At the same time, no true consensus has been reached on what it actually means.

Please take a minute and ask yourself these two questions: First, are you aware of the importance of emotional intelligence to your leadership success? Second (and before reading ahead!), how exactly would you define emotional intelligence? Be specific!

If you're like many leaders, you quickly said yes to the first question, but you struggled to formulate a clear and complete answer to the second question.

For the purposes of mastering our Inner Game of Leadership, I define emotional intelligence as follows:

- Acceptance that emotions are a key driver of all human behavior
- Awareness and acceptance of our own emotions
- The ability to expediently and compassionately navigate our own emotions

- The ability to connect with, understand, and constructively harness our emotions
- The ability to self-soothe when we're upset
- Being able to communicate our emotions in respectful and constructive ways rather than acting them out in disrespectful or destructive ways
- Being able to consciously choose which emotions we show and how we show them

One flaw with the common understanding of emotional intelligence is that we have defined it to include not only navigating our own emotions but also working with the emotions of others. Both are critical skills in becoming unshakeable in our influence, but it's easier to master our Inner Game of Leadership if we conceptualize it differently.

The more helpful way to conceptualize emotional intelligence is to think of it as being about our ability to constructively navigate our own emotions. The navigation of other peoples' emotions is also important, but in my experience, it is largely a separate learning curve that is actually a part of our relational intelligence.

Thus, this chapter details the inner Heartset skills required to work with our own emotions. In the next chapter, Relational Heartset Skills, we will cover the skills related to relational intelligence, including learning to better navigate and harness the emotions of others.

EMOTIONAL INTELLIGENCE SKILL NUMBER ONE: KNOW WHAT YOU ARE FEELING

We've all been culturally conditioned to deny, repress, or otherwise shame ourselves for what we're feeling. In some cultures, this may be more true for men than it is for women, but all genders and nearly all people share some level of this conditioned emotional repression. Thus, the first foundational step to improving our emotional intelligence is to regain a more complete awareness of what emotions we're feeling.

From there, the subsequent emotional intelligence skills sections will build on our increased emotional awareness such that we are able to better navigate, harness, and communicate our emotions in a way that will maximize our influence.

Getting in touch with our emotions can feel scary. For those of us who have kept many of our emotions under lock and key for years, we may worry that we're opening Pandora's box – there's just no telling what kind of pain and difficulty may arise if we go there! For others, we may worry that we will be judged harshly or negatively if we show more of our emotions, so we better keep them under wraps or it's going to come at a dear cost to our career.

Keep in mind that we are social creatures, and we are wired to emotionally connect with each other. Knowing our emotions more deeply will open the door to deeper connection with ourselves and with others. Further, as we rebuild our connection to our own emotions, we are likely to open the door to more connection to something bigger than ourselves – i.e. our purpose is likely to become clearer. In short, we will better motivate and inspire ourselves and others when we are more connected to our emotions.

Becoming more aware of our emotions as adults is a matter of consciously cultivating the habit of checking in with our emotions on a regular basis. Our ability to deepen our awareness of our emotions depends on our Mindset skills of passive meditation and active meditation. We will first use passive meditation to build our emotional awareness in a safe environment. Then, we will begin to apply those same skills in active meditation in our daily lives.

While passively meditating, become more aware of your feelings moment by moment by gently asking yourself this simple question as your mantra: *What am I feeling right now?* Label your emotions as you notice them. Fear. Joy. Sadness. Inspiration. Etc. Just let yourself be passively aware of your emotions with the observer part of your mind. Try not to judge your emotions or attach to them.

As you continue to build this practice in your passive meditation, begin to get more specific in the labeling of your emotions. Find more nuance to the words you use to describe what you're feeling. Are you feeling sad, or are you feeling devastated? Are you feeling joyful, or are you feeling elated? Then, as you go further into building your emotional awareness, ask yourself what other emotions are underneath the initial surface emotions you're noticing. For example, underneath anger is often a feeling of hurt. Underneath that hurt might be the feeling of abandonment. As you grow this practice, begin peeling back the layers of emotions by gently asking yourself what emotion might be underneath this one.

As we cultivate this passive meditation practice more and more, we can then begin to extend our self-questioning to our active meditation practice and check in with ourselves in a similar fashion throughout our day. What am I feeling now? What am I feeling now? And how about now? It's important to cultivate the skill of just noticing our emotions and labeling them. At this stage in our learning curve, we're simply building our emotional awareness and doing nothing new with our emotions.

In the beginning of putting this into practice in our active meditation, we may find ourselves forgetting to check in with our feelings throughout the day. Perhaps an entire day (or even a week or more!) will go by without us checking in with our emotions. First, go easy on yourself if you forget. Talk to yourself as you would talk to your best friend. Second, one thing that I've seen work well to stay on track with this emotional check-in practice is to set a timer on your smartphone with a prompt that pops up every hour or so to remind you to check in with yourself.

Another helpful tactic to gain more awareness of your emotions is to keep a written log of your emotions. Carry a small notepad with you, or perhaps use your smartphone, and just jot down a couple words at a time to record what you're feeling and the time of day you were feeling it. This kind of tracking helps to solidify the habit. Over time, it also helps you to identify any patterns in your feelings. Do I tend to feel frustrated shortly after speaking to my boss? Do I tend to feel angry when meeting with a particular subordinate?

Emotions are rich with information. Among other things, they tell us what to pay attention to. However, for this first foundational step, it's time to just focus on increasing our awareness, expanding our emotional vocabulary, tracking our feelings, and trying not to judge ourselves in any way.

EMOTIONAL INTELLIGENCE SKILL NUMBER TWO: EMOTIONS ARE ALWAYS VALID

The belief that some emotions are good and others are bad runs rampant in today's society. Happiness is good. Sadness is bad. Joy is good. Anger is bad. Love is good. Hate is bad. It's also common to believe that some emotions are normal, and others aren't. In truth, emotions are neither good nor bad, normal nor abnormal. They just are. The simple fact that we feel them means they are real, valid, and normal. Full stop.

Our commonly held judgmental way of conceptualizing emotions is flawed and counter-productive. As soon as we start judging emotions as either good or bad, we are heading down the path of repressing some emotions while over-indulging in other emotions. The way I like to summarize this is to say that the only "bad" emotions are the ones we don't allow ourselves to fully feel, process, and release.

Whether we like it or not, emotions are unstoppable. Any emotions we try to repress will simply find another way to come out of us, and it won't be pretty.

As an analogy, I live in earthquake country in California. I'm no geologist but go with me here. The earth is made up of tectonic plates which often try to move in opposite directions. These plates are typically under friction against each other as they are trying to move in opposite directions. Sometimes the friction doesn't build up much before these plates move. This results in a small, imperceptible shift of the earth's crust, and there's no earthquake that anyone can feel. It's when the friction builds up over a longer period of time and then releases all that pent-up energy in one burst that we have massive earthquakes that destroy buildings and kill people. The 1906 earthquake and resulting fires that pretty much leveled the city of San Francisco is just one example.

Emotions are the same way. There is no possible way to stop them. The only question is: do we release our emotions in small bursts that do no damage, or do we create a catastrophic earthquake of emotion by trying to repress our feelings?

It's when we try to deny our emotions that they are much more likely to come out in unconscious, dysfunctional, and damaging ways. That's why we need to drop our judgmental way of conceptualizing our emotions. Emotions are neither good nor bad. They contain information for us to take into account and nothing more. It is our denial and repression of our emotions that too often turns us into uninspiring and even demotivating leaders.

So, the next skill to work on is this: when you notice your emotions and put labels on them, start to also notice any judgments you have about those emotions. For instance, perhaps you say things to yourself like:

- *I shouldn't be feeling this way.*
- *Oh, that is not normal to feel right now.*
- *I should be happy.*
- *I can't be angry right now.*
- *I don't have time for any emotions right now.*
- *Snap out of it!*
- *I'd better not show any emotions; people might think I'm weak.*
- *I'd better not show any emotions; people might think I'm too emotional.*
- *I'm a woman, so I can't show my emotions in the man's world of business.*
- *Man up!*

Start making notes of the go-to ways in which you unconsciously try to repress your emotions with self-talk judgments. Write them down. Over time, you will likely notice patterns and go-to phrases you say to yourself. Now, use the best friend inner dialog exercise from the self-talk subsection in Chapter 5, Advanced Mindset Skills. Take your usual emotional self-talk and replace it with what you might say to your best friend.

Here are some examples of what you could say to yourself as your own best friend. Experiment and see what works for you:

- *All my emotions are perfectly valid.*
- *I have no bad or wrong emotions.*
- *There are no bad or wrong emotions.*
- *Every emotion that I feel is perfectly normal simply because I feel it.*
- *I can feel my emotions and still be perfectly safe.*
- *My emotions are temporary. This too shall pass.*

It's best to write this down as you will likely struggle to only do this in your head. Once you've captured a list of negative self-talk phrases about your emotions and the best friend phrases you want to replace them with, use your active meditation practice to catch yourself in the act of negative self-talk and replace it with the best friend words.

As you practice this more and more, you will find that you have more awareness of your emotions and more ability to feel them freely. By using these techniques to accept *all* of your emotions with no judgment, you will likely feel lighter on your feet and happier more often. You may even begin to notice that emotions are flowing through you and releasing more quickly and with less unnecessary drama.

Note also that as you become increasingly more in touch with your emotions, you may (at first) feel more emotional more often. You may even have outbursts of emotions all at once. This is not uncommon because you probably have emotions pent up from years of some level of repression. If you're using this exercise and not judging your emotions, those pent-up emotions will now finally be able to release. With these techniques, those pent-up emotions are more likely to simply flow through you without coming out dysfunctionally or in a big earthquake of damage. But consciously take it slowly when you need to. If you notice emotions welling up and wanting to emerge, give yourself time and space to let the emotions flow through you.

EMOTIONAL INTELLIGENCE SKILL NUMBER THREE: TAKE COMPLETE RESPONSIBILITY FOR YOUR FEELINGS

The only person who can make us feel anything is ourselves. As we learned in the Mindset section, it is our interpretations of events – our subjective thoughts about experiences – that create our reality. This, in turn, drives our emotional responses. For example, some people are terrified at the thought of going 170 mph on a motorcycle while others are excited by it. As another example, some people are excited and elated to be a C-Suite leader, and others wouldn't touch that level of responsibility with a ten-foot pole. Some people get excited when involved in interpersonal conflict while others are fearful of it. In all these cases, the circumstances are the same. It's our individual interpretation of the circumstance that creates our emotional response to it.

Anytime we tell ourselves that someone or something is making us feel a certain way we are heading into a victim Mindset on the Drama Paradigm (Chapter 5). Remember that when we are in a victimhood Mindset, we are contributing to perpetuating unnecessary drama. We can shift ourselves off that victim Mindset and into the co-creator Mindset on the Empowerment Paradigm (Chapter 5) when we accept that we control our intellectual and emotional reality with how we interpret events.

That is not to say that others don't play a role in triggering our feelings or that others might not have done something unfair or hurtful to us. Everything is co-created. But what we must focus on to become unshakeable in our influence is that which we have the most control over—ourselves. Only by looking inside ourselves can we develop mastery over our internal narratives, take responsibility for our feelings, choose empowerment over drama, and thereby influence ourselves and others to produce more positive and productive outcomes.

For many, this revelation that we are solely responsible for our feelings is both liberating and scary at the same time. It's liberating because it means we can learn to master our emotions. And it's scary because it means that if we want to obtain that mastery, we must do our inner work and we can no longer blame others. Blame can be comforting because it allows us to avoid taking an honest and hard look inside ourselves. Blame also allows us to avoid acknowledging our own role in emotional reactivity, drama, and dysfunctional communication. Blame also contributes to overly controlling tendencies – if we're blaming others for our emotions, then our next logical step is to try to control others because we believe our emotional experience depends entirely on other people and circumstances. Thus, letting go of our tendency to blame and instead taking responsibility for our feelings is crucial to optimizing our Heartset.

Here are some tips I know work well for learning to take responsibility for our feelings:

- Use *I* language at all times, both internally and externally.
  - For example: I feel angry. I feel hurt. I feel sad. I feel happy. I feel elated.
- Avoid language like:
  - You made me feel ...
  - You made me do this.
  - If only you'd stop doing that thing, I could feel better.
- Recognize that your emotional response is always your responsibility. For example, in the heat of conflict we might say inappropriate, demotivating, or hurtful things. Those are always your responsibility regardless of how much the other person you're in conflict with might also be communicating in disrespectful, unprofessional, or hurtful ways.

And here are some questions to ask yourself to help self-identify when you're not taking responsibility for your feelings:

- Am I blaming someone or something else right now for what I'm feeling?
- How am I responsible for what I'm feeling right now?
- How is my internal, and necessarily subjective, narrative causing me to feel what I'm feeling?

EMOTIONAL INTELLIGENCE SKILL NUMBER FOUR: MINING OUR EMOTIONS FOR USEFUL INFORMATION

In the process of navigating our emotions wisely, it's important to look for the helpful information that our emotions are telling us. For example, if we feel angry, there's a good chance that we believe a boundary of ours has been crossed. Yet when we first feel the anger, we may not know exactly why.

Taking this example further, if we're navigating our own anger wisely, we will:

1. First allow ourselves to fully feel our anger without expressing it outwardly
2. Next ask ourselves where our anger is coming from
3. Then realize that our anger is coming from the fact that we interpreted some sequence of events we witnessed as unfair
4. Next realize (or maybe just recall) that we have a strong value of fair treatment for all
5. Recognize that our interpretation of events could be biased or perhaps based on incomplete information
6. Then inquire within ourselves to better understand what we believe happened and why
7. Then ask others, as appropriate, to reconcile their perceptions of what happened against our own interpretation

8. Finally, make a determination as to what we believe truly happened and take appropriate, mindful action

Notice that it's not until the seventh step of processing our anger that we've taken any outward action. And only at the eighth step do we take any corrective action that might be needed. Also, throughout this whole process we may still be feeling some anger. We don't repress the anger at all; we, instead, channel our anger to productively fuel us through this process rather than blindly reacting or lashing out in anger.

It's common to feel an emotion before we have a conscious understanding of why we're feeling that emotion. Anytime we have an emotional reaction, it's typically because what we wanted and expected to happen either did happen or did not happen. If things did go as we wanted or expected, we're likely to feel emotions like happiness, joy, accomplishment, and contentment. If things did not go as we wanted or expected, we are likely to feel emotions like anger, disappointment, hurt, and sadness. Thus, our emotions can be an early warning signal for something that we need to pay attention to.

Mastering our inner Heartset requires us to look for the useful information that our emotions are conveying to us without being taken over by our emotions and acting rashly. Cultivate the habit of looking for the useful information behind your emotion using similar techniques as described above, and use the emotional intelligence techniques highlighted in this entire chapter to process and release your emotions constructively.

EMOTIONAL INTELLIGENCE SKILL NUMBER FIVE: LEARNING HOW TO SELF-SOOTHE

When you're upset, what do you do?

Do you replay in your mind the scenario that touched one of your emotional triggers, playing yourself up as the victim or perhaps the rescuer/hero? Do you lament what went wrong? Do you wish in your mind that so-and-so didn't treat you this way? Do you say things to yourself like: *How could _____ do this to me? Or I am such a failure! Or I will never get this right!*

Our default behavior toward ourselves when we're emotionally triggered tends to perpetuate a downward spiral of emotion and drama. We tend to judge ourselves and others harshly. We tend to lash out at others with emotions that only escalate the drama. Then we often look for ways to justify our emotional outbursts with more internal and external dialog that casts blame on others, paints ourselves as the victim, and makes others out to be the persecutor/villain of wrong-doing against us. Now the person we feel triggered by has plenty of ammunition for their own version of similar default behaviors that trigger us even more, which triggers a more vehement version of our default behaviors, and the vicious cycle escalates.

Alternatively, we can slow down and take a few breaths. We can tell ourselves that we're doing the best we know how to do in this moment. We can drop judgment and get genuinely curious about why so-and-so is behaving in this way in this moment. We can gently inquire within ourselves as to how we can best respond in order to maximize our influence. We can practice self-compassion while getting curious about why this emotional trigger is coming up for us in this moment. What's the useful information this emotion is trying to convey to me? How can I navigate these emotions constructively and with compassion for myself and others?

In short, when we have a reaction, we can either choose to soothe ourselves such that we can move closer to a calm and grounded state, or we can choose to fan the flames of emotion and reactivity inside of us. It's always a choice, and that choice is always our responsibility, no matter how others around us are behaving.

Here are some self-soothing techniques that I have seen work well:

1. Take a long, slow, deep breath. Make your exhale twice as long as your inhale.

a. Slow deep breaths where the exhale is longer than the inhale have been empirically shown to help induce the parasympathetic response (the opposite of the fight-or-flight response).

b. In your passive meditation practice, you may have sometimes used your breath as a mantra. If so, you can more easily use your breath as a mantra in your active meditation in daily life.

2. Ask yourself, *What is the most inspirational and motivating way for me to respond to this situation?*

3. Know that the only person who can stop you from feeling what you're feeling is you.

4. Get curious about what is happening with the other person whose behavior you are triggered by.

5. Drop judgment of others and assume they're operating from the best of intentions; then try to understand their point of view.

6. Find the truth in what your emotions are telling you. What's the useful information that is present in this emotion?

7. Tell yourself that this is only temporary; it too shall pass.

8. Talk to yourself like you would talk to your best friend.

9. Return to your comfort zone. We will tend to feel the most soothed when we're resting in our comfort zone.

10. If you're proactively practicing meditation, gratitude, and improving your self-talk, you will have a stronger foundation to draw from to soothe yourself. You will also find that you are less likely to become reactive in the first place.

Finally, know that once you find yourself fully emotionally triggered, it can take 20 minutes or more for your body to clear the cortisol and adrenaline of the fight-or-flight response. Once your body is chemically flooded in this way, you may need to step away from the situation so that you can try to come back to it in a calmer state and, thereby, make better decisions as to how to move forward. And, if you do take a break from the situation that triggered you, it's critical that you practice these self-soothing techniques during that break instead of riling yourself up further.

EMOTIONAL INTELLIGENCE SKILL NUMBER SIX: THE 90-SECOND RULE

Here's a fundamental characteristic of emotions that most people don't know: any feeling will pass through our body in 90 seconds or less. But, for most of us, this does not match our experience. Many of us experience our emotions lasting much longer. Why is that?

Two conditions need to be true for an emotion to dissipate within 90 seconds. First, we have to allow ourselves to fully feel the emotion and not deny or repress it in any way. Second, we have to drop the story we're telling ourselves that is triggering the emotion. If any emotion we're experiencing is not subsiding within 90 seconds, then we're not doing one or both of these two things.

Remember that however irrational or disproportionate our emotional reaction might be, the emotion itself is always real and valid. If we judge the emotion in any way, try to rationally understand it before we allow ourselves to feel it, or in any other way repress it, that emotion will likely linger longer than 90 seconds. Perhaps a lot longer. We must get out of our judgmental head and into our non-judgmental heart and just let the emotion flow.

Also remember that our emotions are created by our thoughts. It is our mental interpretation of what happened that leads us to feel a certain way. This is good because our emotions can be early warning signals of something we need to pay attention to. It's when we internally repeat our interpretation of what happened again and again that we re-trigger the same emotion again and again. Thus, this is the only other way that emotions can persist longer than 90 seconds. We may experience it as a continuous emotion, yet we're actually triggering the emotion again and again by re-living the experience and our interpretation of what it means to us.

And quite often, when we are repeating that story and re-living the event, the story we're telling ourselves depicts things in one of two ways: 1) It paints ourselves as a victim and another as a persecutor/villain; or 2) It paints ourselves as a rescuer/hero and another as a victim, while perhaps a third party is involved as the persecutor/villain. Both of these types of stories put us firmly on the Drama Paradigm; thus, they only cause us to perpetuate drama and disempowerment.

Note that not all stories we internally paint will necessarily depict ourselves in these ways, but it is quite common. When you find yourself in a thought-loop around a given event, in all likelihood you are depicting things in one of these two ways. And that distorted and self-centered story you're repeating to yourself is keeping you trapped in a never-ending cycle of reactivity and drama, thereby undermining your influence as a leader.

So, what do we do when we find ourselves feeling a strong emotion and perhaps beginning to feel the fight-or-flight response taking over?

- Remind yourself that you cannot think clearly if you don't release your emotions.
- Let your emotions flow through your body with no judgment or repression.
- Perhaps use some techniques highlighted in the self-soothing section.
- Look for the useful information in the emotion, but don't let the emotion run you.
- Look at the stories you're telling yourself. Are you on the Drama Paradigm? If so, use some of the tools in that section to shift yourself to the Empowerment Paradigm.
- Remind yourself to let go of any stories you're telling yourself and just feel your feelings.
- Remember that there are dysfunctional and functional ways to release your emotions, as you will see in the next section.

EMOTIONAL INTELLIGENCE SKILL NUMBER SEVEN: HOW TO RELEASE EMOTIONS PRODUCTIVELY AND CONSTRUCTIVELY

One of the crux points of optimizing our Heartset is mastering the ability to release all our emotions productively and constructively.

But first let's review all the skills of emotional intelligence:

- Learning to be fully aware of what we're feeling
- Cultivating the ability to fully feel our feelings without judgment or attachment
- Taking complete responsibility for our feelings
- Mining the emotion for its useful information
- Self-soothing as needed
- Letting go of our distorted, internal stories
- Releasing our emotions productively and constructively
- And then consciously choosing the action we take, including what emotions to show and how to show them

Once we've deepened emotional intelligence skills one through six, we can begin cultivating the skill of consciously expressing what we're feeling in a productive way. For example, let's say we're talking 1:1 with a subordinate who is currently under-performing. In the course of this conversation, our subordinate is clearly making excuses for their under-performance. We have a belief that people should always take responsibility for getting their job done, and we have a low tolerance for what comes across to us as making excuses for bad performance. This pisses us off.

In that moment, we have a choice. We can give in to our anger and repeat the story inside ourselves about how this person is continually making excuses and playing the role of the victim. This will in turn incite us to play the role of either rescuer/hero or persecutor/villain – and now the interaction is firmly on the Drama Paradigm, and we're *both* perpetuating reactivity and drama. But we don't know this yet, so our inner anger grows as we repeat the internal story of this person being a slacker and not taking responsibility. From that place of escalating inner anger, we're beginning to experience the fight-or-flight response, and our ability to empathize, think creatively, or be curious about the other person is greatly diminished.

We then snap at this person in an aggressive fashion and say something like, "You're just making excuses for your poor performance. This is what you always do rather than looking at your bad performance. You blame everything and everyone else. It's time for you to just suck it up and get the job done. No more excuses!"

This way of interacting with the subordinate will likely lead him to conclude that we're a jerk. He's not likely to feel motivated. He's likely to believe that his boss doesn't really care about him and just wants him to perform to unrealistic standards. From that belief, he may under-perform even more. Let's also look at the words here. There's nothing actionable or constructive in what we've said. We've simply been uncivil to this person, and we have already seen in detail the demoralizing effects uncivil behavior has on employees.

A different choice we could make in that moment is to pause and notice our anger rising; we could let ourselves feel the anger without judging it or showing it outwardly. We then notice the story we start to tell ourselves about this person always making excuses. We next recognize our internal dialog as containing the key word "always," an indicator to us that our thinking is likely distorted. We then say to ourselves that he doesn't *always* do this, but it is a bit of a pattern that we need to address.

Then we ask ourselves, *What is the best way for me to hold this person accountable? How can I give him this feedback in a productive way that motivates him rather than demoralizes him?* We feel ourselves calming down as we have this inner dialog. From that calmer place, we now remember that this person is very sensitive to criticism. That annoys us because we think of ourselves as thick-skinned, and we start getting angry again. However, then we pause again, take a deep breath with a longer exhale than inhale, and ask ourselves, *How can I best motivate* **him**, *not* **me**?

From this place of consciously choosing how to use our anger, we then say in a firm, but compassionate voice, "I've noticed when we talk about your performance not meeting expectations, you sometimes get defensive, and it seems like you're making excuses. I recognize that there are many variables in your projects and you're not directly responsible for all of them, but when you make a commitment to me and the team, I expect you to live up to that commitment. If for any reason something changes, and you can't make the deadline, I need you to tell me right away so we can course correct as soon as possible. I want to support you here and help you get that promotion that we talked about in June. This is an area we need to work on to get you ready for that next level... Can you tell me what gets in your way when it comes to living up to the commitments you've made to me and the team?"

From here, our subordinate is likely to believe that we want to help them to help themselves. They are likely to feel championed and held accountable at the same time. The dialog continues, only in a more constructive way than our default reaction would have led to.

Notice the difference in our inner dialog here. We're working with ourselves every step of the way. We didn't have our emotions all handled immediately; we processed it as we were in the conversation. We took our time and slowed down when we needed to. We self-soothed and got curious about how we can best motivate this person while still holding them accountable. As a result, the ensuing conversation was constructive, and that subordinate is more likely to up their game to be more productive, engaged, and communicative going forward.

EMOTIONAL INTELLIGENCE SKILL NUMBER EIGHT: CHOOSING THE EMOTIONS YOU SHOW

As you expand your emotional intelligence practice, you will begin to realize that you often experience multiple emotions simultaneously.

You might even notice that you sometimes feel seemingly conflicting emotions at the same time. For instance, you might feel angry, hurt, and sad while also feeling a tinge of joy. Other times, you might be excited, anxious, and exuberant all at once. And still other times you might feel bored, restless, and loving all at once.

This may be confusing when it first starts to happen for you, but it's perfectly normal. It's also a sign that you're progressing into more advanced capabilities with your emotional intelligence. With this more advanced emotional awareness, you can now start to experiment with choosing which emotions you show. The practice of doing this requires you to be as aware as possible of your emotions. It also requires you to play with the internal narrative that triggers your emotions. You can use that internal narrative to help emphasize the emotion you want to emphasize in the moment.

For example, if you want to emphasize some sadness you're feeling in order to create a poignant moment, listen to your internal dialog that's feeding that sadness. Maybe you're sad about your son going off to college soon. Imagine him being gone, not hearing from him often, and how you expect to feel in response to that. Now you've got some more sadness to work with for your upcoming conversation with a peer who is also going through a sad experience with losing a loved one.

The goal, of course, is to maximize your influence by consciously choosing which emotions you show and when and how you show them. In addition to emphasizing the emotions you're already feeling, you can cultivate emotions inside of you in a similar fashion as a method actor. For example, a while back I was getting ready to step on stage to share a talk with a sales force at their annual sales kick-off meeting. I wanted to be as happy, emotive, and high energy as possible. But I'm an introvert by nature, so I'm not typically bubbling over with lots of visible enthusiasm. I also hadn't gotten much sleep the night before this particular event due to travel difficulties, so I was really dragging.

To get myself ready for this moment, I recalled my first motorcycle racing victory. I replayed it in my head moment-by-moment as I approached the finish line and took the checkered flag. I recalled how excited and accomplished I felt as I crossed the finish line in first place. And, finally, I recalled how elated I felt for days and weeks afterward. As I took the stage, I imagined I had just won that race that morning. In so doing, I was able to conjure the energy I wanted to bring to that audience and had a great time doing it.

If you're just getting started in your emotional intelligence practice, you might have a hard time believing that you could consciously cultivate specific emotions within yourself. You may also find it hard to believe that you could ever have the capacity to notice multiple emotions inside of you at the same time. You can do it. It's largely a matter of consistent practice, utilizing all of our skills such as self-compassion, active and passive meditation, and improving our self-talk.

If you ever feel overwhelmed or like this is too much to do on your own, or perhaps these exercises stir up some old, emotional trauma that you'd like some help with, please do at least reach out to a trusted friend or loved one to talk things through. Also, consider hiring a good executive coach or psychotherapist to help you work through these skills and anything that might arise as you practice them. When it comes to working toward being the best version of ourselves, that kind of assistance can be invaluable.

Chapter 9

Relational Heartset Skills

IF YOU DO AN internet search on communication skills, you will find more than a billion articles, books, videos, etc. Communication skills matter, but what has not received anywhere near enough attention is the inner game of how we communicate and relate to others.

This chapter is not about communication skills as that is already well-covered by other available resources. This chapter instead focuses on how we can become more unshakeable in our influence by taking a deep dive into who we are being when we relate to others, the choices we make in how we relate to others, and how we can best navigate and harness the emotions of others.

PRACTICING EXQUISITE SELF-CARE

I'm sure most of us have been on airplanes and heard the flight attendants go through the safety instructions before the plane takes off. But few of us have really allowed ourselves to absorb the meaning of this statement: "Put your own oxygen mask on first before assisting others." The idea, of course, is that if we're passed out from lack of oxygen due to not taking care of ourselves first, we cannot possibly help anyone else. The concept of taking care of ourselves first, in order to be capable of taking better care of others, applies in all contexts and not just in case of emergency on an airplane.

In a leadership context, lack of proper self-care leads to more reactivity, more stress, more mistakes, more mood swings, less effective communication, less presence, and overall a lessened ability to function at our best. Further, in times of unusually high stress, self-care is often one of the first things that gets sacrificed, and it is likely to be a downward spiral from there. Self-care is not a luxury we can disregard as soon as things get demanding. It's precisely when things are the hardest that we need to practice self-care the most.

Self-care is not to be confused with being selfish. Self-care is actually a way to best support ourselves in being of optimal service to everyone. Practicing exquisite self-care is a crucial foundational skill for mastering our Inner Game of Leadership as it greatly impacts both our Mindset and our Heartset.

Exquisite self-care includes:

- Carving out time for ourselves
- Quality time with loved ones
- Regular exercise
- Sufficient restorative sleep
- Eating well
- Having fun doing things we love
- Staying hydrated
- Not excessively drinking alcohol or abusing other substances
- Doing the things that make us feel great
- Finding humor in everything, especially the mundane
- Listening to our favorite music
- Playing music or singing, if that's our thing

We Are Manipulating Each Other All the Time

One of the most common ways in which people push back on the concept of mastering their emotions and consciously choosing which emotions to show is to protest that they don't want to be manipulative. They believe that conscious mastery over emotions – and especially consciously choosing their emotional state – is somehow not fully authentic. And from that belief, it's easy to conclude that emotional intelligence can be a form of manipulation.

My answer to that protest is always the same – you're right; it is manipulative. We are all manipulating each other all the time. We're all trying to get what we want, and we very often need the cooperation of others to get what we want. The only real questions are these: How consciously do we want to approach getting what we want? What is our intent behind our "manipulation"? Is our intent to get what we want at any cost regardless of how it impacts others? Or is our intent to get what we want while also respecting what other people want, all in an effort to move toward a better outcome for everyone?

In short, the distinction to pay attention to is our own intentions behind our actions. If we're genuinely focused on achieving the best outcomes for everyone, then we're not being manipulative when we work intelligently with our emotions to maximize our influence over ourselves and others. If the intent behind our actions is not above board or is overly self-serving, that's when we're getting off track.

What I like to say is that our Heartset skills, including emotional intelligence, are simply tools. Like any other tool, the tool itself is completely neutral. It can either be used for good or for evil – the choice is ours. Let's use our improved Heartset wisely and with compassion.

We Are the Product of the People We Are Closest To. Let's Choose Wisely.

As we shift our Mindset and Heartset into a more empowering and influential view of ourselves and the world, we will be changing – perhaps rapidly at times. This may be disorienting, and a part of us may crave the comfort of the familiar. Remember: if we are to be successful in mastering our Inner Game of Leadership, we need to get comfortable being uncomfortable. Nowhere does our need for comfort come on more strongly than in our relationships with those closest to us. But in times of growth, those closest to us may struggle to accept and support us in our new growth.

We can't avoid the fact that by changing ourselves, we are changing the relational dynamics with everyone we know. Imagine what it's like for the important people in our lives. They have to adjust to a new version of us. They didn't choose that change—we did. As a result, they may resist, or perhaps even unconsciously try to sabotage, the new and improved version of us. One of our biggest enemies to success in improving ourselves is our environment – including most of all the important people in our lives. When others, especially those with whom we are the closest, resist us improving ourselves, we may be tempted to give up because it seems too costly on our relationships.

Jim Rohn, an entrepreneur, author, and motivational speaker once said that we are the product of the five people we are closest to. If we are to be successful in making significant changes in our lives, we need to be prepared to enroll and influence the people around us to at least support us in our pursuit of leadership excellence and perhaps even join us on the journey. If they refuse and don't learn to welcome our growth, we need to ask ourselves some serious questions about that relationship and how we want to be with that person going forward. Perhaps we are outgrowing that relationship, and it's time to let it go, or perhaps there's a new way for us to relate that enables us to continue to grow, or perhaps we still maintain that relationship but it becomes more distant.

Letting go of, or redefining, relationships can be painful. But by letting go of people who no longer fit in our lives, we are making room for new relationships with new people who do fit and who will support us in an upward spiral of our growth and theirs. If we settle for anything less than that, we will be undermining our ability to grow. We are social creatures, and we are deeply influenced by those around us, especially those we are closest to. Let us choose our closest relationships wisely and recognize that some of the relationship choices the old version of us made may not fit with the new version of ourselves we're growing into.

This may sound selfish or perhaps even cold. It's not. Remember: we have to put our own oxygen mask on first to be able to best support and influence others to step into their greatness. If we feel like we've outgrown a relationship, the other person is probably feeling that disconnect too, at least at some level. It's likely better for both of us to let go or at least redefine how we're going to be together. This is an advanced Heartset skill because it takes courage, awareness, compassion, relationship-focus, and determination to shift relationships to being more supportive of our best self.

Many of us unconsciously stop here because redefining or giving up some of the closest relationships we have seems daunting and scary. But if we don't learn to treat our leadership growth as one of the biggest rocks in our lives, and thereby ensure we honor and defend our growth with everything we've got, we will certainly hold ourselves back. Nowhere is that more important than in choosing whom we are closest to.

PRACTICING DISCERNMENT INSTEAD OF JUDGMENT

When it comes to relating to ourselves and others in a way that brings out the best in us, there is an important distinction to be drawn between discernment and judgment.

We need to make judgments in order to make decisions in life. When making hiring decisions, we need to judge who is the best fit. When kicking off a project, we need to judge who to include on that project. When deciding on the best company strategy, we need to judge which strategy will best serve the company's goals. Judgment is good – up to a point.

It's when we begin to equate a person's overall worthiness with a specific judgment in a specific area that judgment becomes problematic. Someone may not be the right fit for the role we're hiring for, but that doesn't mean they are fundamentally inferior in any way.

Someone may not be particularly skilled at leadership, but that doesn't make them fundamentally inferior in any way. A strategy that doesn't fit our company at this time might be the best possible strategy for another company or another time.

Judgment feels personal. When a person is communicating from an internal Heartset of judgment, the subtext of that communication often suggests that you – as a person – fall short. Judgment is based on a fixed Mindset. Recall from Carol Dweck's work that a fixed mindset is the belief that a person's skills, knowledge, and abilities cannot change. Therefore, if their skills aren't a good match for our needs, we are more likely to judge them to be inferior as a person.

Discernment, on the other hand, is the practice of making decisions based on the concept of best fit. Discernment feels different than judgment because it includes no Heartset of hierarchy. It includes no concept or suggestion that anyone is better-than or less-than anyone else. Discernment is based on the growth Mindset. A growth Mindset, as you may recall, is the belief that everyone can learn, grow, and change.

Discernment feels better. More importantly, discernment motivates and inspires, while judgment demotivates and discourages. That is because when we communicate from an internal Heartset of judgment, we communicate to others that there is a hierarchy of who's good and who's bad. Further, judgment feels permanent and cold, and discourages anyone who falls short from doing anything about it. Discernment feels temporary and compassionate and, therefore, encourages people to step up and grow into the person they need to be to get what they want.

SAYING NO IN ORDER TO SAY YES

Former United Kingdom Prime Minister Tony Blair once said, "The art of leadership is saying no, not saying yes."

One of the hardest things for us to do is to say no to another human being. We tend to be so afraid of disappointing others, so afraid of missing out on something, so afraid of not measuring up to some nebulous yet exacting standard of doing it all, that we struggle to say no. As a result, over-commitment and under-delivery are the norm these days. Worse, we tend to fill our jars with sand and pebbles, and the big rocks – the most important things – get crowded out. All because of the all-too-common fear of saying no.

The fear of saying no to something or someone is probably the biggest human factor in why so many organizations have "strategies" that involve way too many things. As a result, many company strategies read more like to-do lists. Too many competing priorities create confusion, overwhelm, and inaction (or at least slow-as-molasses action) at an organization-wide level.

Let's look at the turnaround of Apple as a key example. In the late 1990's, Apple had clearly lost the hard-fought battle for supremacy in the personal computer market to its arch-rival Microsoft. In 1997, Apple had been hemorrhaging money for a dozen years with an increasingly bloated product line, a number of key commercial failures, and some costly strategic mistakes such as betting on the PowerPC chipset. In short, Apple was on the verge of bankruptcy and seemed completely unsavable.

In July 1997, Steve Jobs took over the company as interim CEO. By September 1997, Jobs had cut 70% of the company's product line and had formed an unpopular, yet ultimately crucial, partnership with Microsoft. In 1998, Apple introduced the iMac – its first smashing commercial success in years. This marked the beginning of a tremendous financial turnaround that ultimately resulted in Apple becoming the first company with a market capitalization that exceeded one trillion US dollars in 2018.

Steve Jobs once quipped, "Focusing is about saying no." He also said, "That's been one of my mantras – focus and simplicity. Simple can be harder than complex; you have to work hard to get your thinking clean to make it simple." Apple's journey from 1997 until 2019 has included lots of new product innovations and some failures along the way, but the successes (like the iPod, iTunes, iPad, and iPhone) have far outweighed the failures. What is perhaps most remarkable is that Apple's mantra since 1997 has remained the same: Be obsessively focused on doing a few things exceptionally well, always with an eye to keeping products meaningful, simple, beautiful, and easy to use. This strategy has paid huge dividends for Apple and its shareholders.

So how does this relate to optimizing our Heartset? We struggle to say no largely because we're afraid of disappointing others. But when we fail to say no to the wrong (or less important) things, we no longer can say yes to the most important things. Recall the story from Chapter 2 where we saw the need to put our big rocks in our jar first or we will never be able to get to our big rocks at all. Putting our big rocks in our jar first requires that we become comfortable saying no a whole lot more often than we say yes.

It's a costly mistake to say yes when we should say no. The more we optimize our Mindset and Heartset as unshakeable leaders, the more we will feel confident in saying no when we need to.

DON'T PUT ANYONE ON A PEDESTAL (AND BE WARY OF ANYONE WHO PUTS US ON A PEDESTAL)

It's one thing to admire and honor someone else's achievements, position, or power. It's something else to intellectually or emotionally put that person above us – on a pedestal as the saying goes.

Imagine working at a large, multi-national corporation and approaching your company's CEO to speak with him 1:1 for the first time. You know that you only get one chance at a first impression, and that first impression with the CEO could change your life for the better in a big way. Conversely, making a poor first impression could have the opposite impact on your life. What are you feeling as you walk into the CEO's office? Anxious? Scared? Excited? Is your mouth dry with worry? What thoughts are going through your mind? Are you intimidated? Are you feeling less-than in the presence of someone in such a powerful role? Do you believe that people in such positions of power are fundamentally smarter, better educated, or somehow more special than you are?

In today's society, these are all pretty common thoughts and feelings to have in this scenario. And they are signs that we tend to put people in power on a pedestal.

When we put someone on a pedestal, we devalue ourselves and overvalue the other person. As a result, the power dynamics between us become skewed in an unhealthy way. This is dangerous territory. As long as we place people on pedestals, we will struggle to see them as the flawed human beings that we all are. We will tend to think they can do no wrong. We will overvalue their words and actions. We will give away our power in their presence.

Or perhaps you have an assumption that those in positions of power are too wealthy, too out of touch, and maybe even corrupt. This is actually the same way of thinking; however, instead of putting someone else on a pedestal, we are putting ourselves on a pedestal. Instead of thinking of the CEO as somehow better than us, we're thinking of ourselves as better than the CEO. We're elevating ourselves in an unhealthy way that will also prevent us from showing up as our best selves. We will likely come across as arrogant, superior, and not a team player.

This goes back to practicing discernment instead of judgment. Certainly, some people have some skills, experiences, and natural gifts that others don't have. That fact does not make anyone fundamentally better than anyone else. To maximize our influence, we need to come from a foundational Heartset and Mindset that everyone deserves equal respect simply because they're human.

Putting someone on a pedestal is also dangerous because we will not be able to function at our best when we're around this person. We will worry about saying the "right" thing or the "wrong" thing. We may bend over backwards to try to impress this person, perhaps compromising our values in the process. These behaviors also signal to ourselves and to others that we don't have as much composure as we could have when in the presence of those in power. Becoming unshakeable in our influence means consciously cultivating our ability to be fully present and highly functioning in all circumstances, especially high-stakes circumstances like meeting with a CEO.

Further, with anyone we have put on a pedestal, we are likely to eventually find reasons to tear them down. When we tear someone down from the pedestal, we will tend to go from thinking they can do nothing wrong to thinking they can do nothing right. In psychological terms, this is called "splitting." Splitting is the tendency to conceptualize people in black and white terms and, therefore, to have difficulty reconciling the positive and negative qualities of a person into a cohesive whole. Not coincidentally, when we conceptualize others in black-and-white terms, we tend to also conceptualize ourselves in black/white terms. This black-and-white thinking tends to create mood swings and emotional volatility and is another factor that contributes to our never-ending cycles of reactivity.

We all have some tendency to view ourselves and others in black-and-white terms. It's a mental and emotional habit that starts when we are children. At that young and tender age, we have a psychological need to see our caregivers in an idealized way. We must do this because we are so completely dependent on them for love, affection, and sustenance. Without their support, we simply could not stay alive. Thus, rather than think that our caregivers might be flawed (and therefore not 100% reliable as caregivers), we put them on a pedestal. We must do this for our healthy psychological development as children.

As we mature into adulthood and beyond, we must begin to accept that everyone is flawed. We need to learn the skill of reconciling seemingly dichotomous tendencies in our parents and in all human beings. We need to learn to integrate everyone's positive and negative traits into a cohesive whole and recognize that no one is either all good or all bad. We're all a mixture of both.

As we get better and better at mastering the Inner Game of Leadership, we will become more prominent and more influential. As a result, we will attract more people who will put us on a pedestal. We need to be as wary of anyone putting us on a pedestal as we are of putting others on a pedestal for all the same reasons. Elevating us to an exalted status will likely prevent them from being totally honest with us. They will struggle to own their personal power while in our presence and, as a result, they will be less effective. And at some point, they may find a reason to tear us down from that pedestal and suddenly go from believing we can do nothing wrong to believing that we can do nothing right.

Believe it or not, the tendency to put others on a pedestal is actually a form of blame and not taking full responsibility for ourselves. If our belief system includes the idea that certain people are fundamentally better than us and deserve to be put on a pedestal, then we necessarily let ourselves off the hook from owning our own greatness. It can be an excuse to play small, telling ourselves that we're just not like those great, god-like, people who are on pedestals. By wallowing in our belief that we're not one of those great people, we will prevent ourselves from ever being able to live into our own inherent greatness.

BE WILLING TO ADMIT THAT WE DON'T HAVE ALL THE ANSWERS

Saying "I don't know" is one of the most difficult things for many leaders to say, yet it is sometimes the most powerful response a leader can give.

As we've touched on already, we have been conditioned to avoid the possibility of looking ignorant or incompetent. Therefore, it's easy for us to default to feigning knowledge we don't actually have or at least are not that sure about. The problem is that if we pretend to know the answer to something that we don't know, people will tend to believe us! As a result, an important question will get an incorrect or incomplete answer. That can lead the team and even the organization off in the wrong direction. Further, by pretending to know something we don't know, we undermine and devalue the expertise of those around us. In doing so, we likely preempt anyone else on the team who may actually have a solid answer to the question from chiming in with their knowledge and expertise. Finally, we set an example that communicates to everyone that they'd better feign knowledge even when they don't have it. This is dangerous territory.

It's not a weakness to admit we don't know everything. No one person could possibly know everything. It's a leadership strength to acknowledge that we don't know everything. It creates an example of emotional and intellectual honesty that many organizations could use more of.

From a leadership and relational perspective, if we don't know the answer to something, let's be willing to say so. If it's something we need to know the answer to, then let's stay silent and let others chime in, or ask others who have the expertise to find the answer, or commit to finding the answer ourselves.

EXECUTIVE PRESENCE

Executive presence is a term that gets thrown around a lot these days. Most of us recognize executive presence when we see it, but can we define it? What does executive presence actually mean? Take a minute and formulate your best answer to this question.

When people answer this question, they typically speak in terms of the impact of someone who has great executive presence. They talk about things like influence, enrolling people in a vision, and inspiring people to action. They may also talk about things like charisma, allure, and magnetism.

Many of us assume we either have executive presence or we don't. Even the words above, charisma, allure, and magnetism, suggest that we're either born with these characteristics or we're not. It may be true that some level of charisma is present at birth. It may also be true that some people have had childhood, school, or work experiences that have better supported them in developing their executive presence. And most importantly, executive presence can be learned. In fact, everyone I know with great executive presence only got there with lots of mindful practice and often also some mentorship and coaching along the way.

Executive presence is nothing more than bringing the full force of our complete mind, heart, body, and spirit to the current moment. Put another way, executive presence is being in a peak state while being fully present in the current moment.

And in case you haven't noticed, that's exactly what mastering our Inner Game of Leadership is all about. Executive presence is one of the key outcomes of becoming unshakeable in our influence. All we need to do is stay the course by doing our inner work highlighted in this book, getting the help we need along the way and, above all, maintaining a deep commitment to never giving up on ourselves and our inner growth as leaders.

MEET PEOPLE WHERE THEY'RE AT

Before we can effectively influence anyone to go somewhere new with us, we must first meet them where they're at. Everyone has a fundamental need to feel that they are seen, heard, and valued for who they are and what they contribute. Not who they might be in the future or what they might contribute in the future, but who they are right here, right now.

That's why - believe it or not - the person who speaks the least in a meeting can have the most influence. If we don't first understand, empathize with, and accept other people's words, they will more likely resist being influenced by us. That's why the best way to get people to listen to us and be influenced by us is often to first listen to them. We must *make it a priority to try to understand others before trying to be understood.* Then we take that understanding and weave it together with our own beliefs and create a win-win that people can more easily get behind.

At a high level, this is achieved by:

1. Listening to everyone and demonstrating that we understand their perspectives
2. Remaining genuinely open to being influenced by others

3. Openly acknowledging when our position changes due to someone else's influence
4. Taking everyone's perspectives (including our own), putting them in the context of the bigger picture, and enrolling people in a win-win that is best for everyone

We have to remember that people want to connect. One of the key ways that we connect (or not) with others is by determining if they are similar to us or not. If we perceive that another person is similar to us, then we will likely feel more connected to them. When we are more connected to someone, we are far more open to being influenced by them.

Trying to understand before trying to be understood is a classic situation of giving first, and it often pays huge dividends in our ability to influence others. We can't fake it, but we can choose to show genuine curiosity and concern for others and then really listen to them.

Conscious Heart-Based Listening

When we think of listening, we typically conceptualize it in a one-dimensional fashion as simply hearing what another person is saying. But that is only one of three dimensions of listening.

The three dimensions of listening are:

- Listening to ourselves
- Listening to others
- Listening to the overall environment we're operating in

It's important to be aware that all three dimensions of listening are actually directly related to maximizing our connection to ourselves, maximizing our connection to others, and maximizing our connection to something bigger than ourselves.

The first dimension of listening, listening to ourselves, is directly related to the primary argument of this book: we will maximize our influence and leadership ability by cultivating the best possible relationship we can have with ourselves – i.e. by mastering our Inner Game of Leadership. Thus, many of the skills highlighted in this book include listening to ourselves.

For example, our Mindset skills of meditation, self-compassion, and improving our self-talk all involve listening to ourselves more deeply. Additionally, all our inner Heartset skills in navigating our own emotions involve listening to ourselves more deeply. Our improved ability to listen to ourselves will drive a deeper connection to ourselves and, thus, fuel us to do our best work.

The second dimension of listening, listening to others, is critical to our relational Heartset skills and constitutes perhaps the most important relational Heartset element of mastering our Inner Game of Leadership. It will drive deeper connection with others, and that will tend to cause both us and others to do our best work.

Listening to another person includes more than just paying attention to the words they're saying. Remember that about 60-80% of the information being conveyed is non-verbal. For example, here are some specific things to be listening for:

- What is their body language communicating?
- What are their facial expressions saying?
- What does their eye contact tell you about their culture, personality and/or sensitivity of what they're communicating?
- What does their posture tell you?
- What does the tone of their voice tell you? Are they using a wide variety of tones, or are they monotone?
- What does their vocal volume tell you? Are they whispering? Are they shouting?
- Does this seem like a difficult thing for them to say, or is it rolling off their tongue like it's the easiest thing in the world?
- Are they animated and excited, or do they seem bored?
- Do they seem anxious?

All these factors communicate volumes about what is going on with someone. The key is listening mindfully and paying close attention to pick up on these details. And to do that, we've got to have our mind and heart relatively quiet when we listen. If we're having a strong emotional reaction, our listening ability will be diminished. If we're thinking about what we want to say or what we think while also trying to listen, we're pulling our attention away from actually listening. At some level, the other person will sense that we're not fully present with them and will feel less heard and less valued. They may even feel disrespected because we're not truly listening.

To fully listen, we want to listen with our mind, our heart, and our body – i.e. our entire presence.

Here are some specific tips for conscious and heart-based listening to another person:

1. **Mindset and Heartset are required to listen effectively:**
   a. Clear your mind and heart.
      i. Manage your own reactions and do not let them get in the way of listening.
      ii. Be willing to at least set aside your reactions and thoughts long enough to listen effectively.
   b. Exhibit genuine curiosity about the other person.
   c. Be willing to focus your complete attention on the other person.
   d. Be ready to defer any judgment and just listen.
2. **How to listen, step-by-step:**
   a. Ask an open-ended question with genuine curiosity.
   b. Listen carefully.
      i. Don't interject with related stories of your own.
      ii. Only say affirming things (note that you don't have to agree).
   c. Show that you're listening with your body language, for example:
      i. Nod occasionally.

   ii. Lean forward in an engaged fashion.

   iii. Make eye contact (be mindful of cultural norms here).

 d. Imagine and try to tune in to what this person is feeling at that moment.

   i. You can say things like:

    1. Did you feel angry about that?

    2. I'm guessing that was frustrating for you. Was it?

    3. Wow! That sounds disappointing.

    4. How did that make you feel?

    5. Wow! That probably felt great. What was that like for you?

 e. Ask clarifying questions, as needed. For example:

   i. Can you say more about that so I can make sure I understand?

 f. Ask for a pause to paraphrase what you've heard.

   i. Let me repeat back to you what I think you're saying, so I can make sure I understand.

   ii. Did I get that right?

    1. If yes, great. Continue.

    2. If no, ask what you missed.

 g. Before concluding, ask if they feel heard and understood.

   i. If not, ask what you've missed and continue until they feel heard.

 h. Close by acknowledging them for what they shared with you.

   i. A simple and sincere "thank you" will often work well.

The feeling of being heard, valued, and respected is a powerful impact to have on others. That's why conscious and heart-based listening is a foundational skill for maximizing our relational Heartset. As we master this skill, people will open up more, trust us more, and be more open to influence by us. They will also feel more connected to us and will likely do better work as a result.

Finally, the third dimension of listening is to listen to the environment within which we are operating. If we're in a meeting, for example, this level of listening would include paying attention to the collective group in the meeting. What's the prevalent emotional tone of the group as a whole, moment by moment? Is it anticipation? Excitement? Joy? Humor? Somberness? Anxiety? Fear? And on a larger scale, we're listening to the environment that goes beyond the meeting itself. For example, we also need to pay attention to the backdrop within the entire company at the time. Did the company just announce horrible financial results from the most recent quarter and people are generally worried and stressed about that? Or did we just have an incredible IPO and there's huge excitement in the air?

By consciously paying attention to this dimension, we can make better decisions about how to communicate to maximize our influence. We can consciously blend in with the current mood of the room with what we say and how we say it. We can ask ourselves if the current emotional energy in the room is optimal. If not, we can take steps to change the energy for the better.

For instance, if the room seems overly serious, we can make a joke to lighten the mood. In doing so, people are likely to become more expressive, open, and creative. Conversely, if the mood seems too jovial and people are not taking things seriously enough, we can interject with an appropriate, somber story to get people to focus on solving a difficult problem at hand. By focusing on this dimension of listening, we will also tend to feel more connected to something bigger than ourselves. This connection tends to cause us to feel more purposeful and, thereby, more likely to do our best work.

As unshakeable leaders, we need to be paying attention on all three of these dimensions at all times; however, there may be times when we're justifiably more focused on one dimension than another. Most of us find it easiest to get started doing this in a sequential fashion: first, we listen to ourselves; next, we listen to another; then we listen to the environment. We simply repeat that sequence. As we gain more confidence and skill, we will start to jump around between these dimensions at will depending on which dimension of listening most needs our attention right now.

HOW TO NAVIGATE OTHER PEOPLE'S EMOTIONS

Our ability to constructively navigate and harness the power of other people's emotions is directly proportionate to our ability to first do that for ourselves. That's because the more we understand the depths of our own emotions and how to best work with them, the more we will know how to do that with other people. Additionally, it's important to have some level of mastery over our own emotional reactions before we can effectively and constructively focus on the emotions of others. For this reason, we worked on our inner Heartset skills first (in Chapter 8).

In this section, we will take what we learned in Chapter 8 and use the same techniques in the same order; this time, however, we're learning to apply these skills to other people and not just ourselves.

SKILL ONE: KNOW WHAT THEY ARE FEELING

To navigate the emotions of others, we must first be aware of the emotions of others. Before we can amplify our awareness of other people's emotions, we must become skilled at soothing ourselves such that we're not in a strong reaction or emotion ourselves. So with all skills related to navigating and harnessing the emotions of others, we must first get ourselves into a relatively calm state. Please refer to Chapter 8 to refresh on techniques for how to do this.

In the context of knowing what others are feeling, it's important to distinguish between empathy and sympathy. Empathy is our ability to feel the feelings of another person. Sympathy is our ability to cognitively recognize another person's emotions without actually feeling them.

We are born with both of these abilities. Recall from Chapter 8 how we are wired to emotionally attune to others, starting with our primary caregivers. Recall also how we tend to automatically mirror other people's emotions. And, finally, remember how we tend to do our best work when we feel the most connected. These are all related to just how social we are as a species. Thus, the ability to tune into another's emotions is more about unleashing our natural abilities in these areas than it is about learning anything new.

When it comes to tuning into another's emotions, empathy and sympathy are both useful tools. Empathy can work very well for quickly getting in touch with another's feelings, but it has risks. Empathy can sometimes lead to us feeling another person's feeling so strongly that we become overwhelmed. If we are overwhelmed with another's emotion, it will be harder for us to be effective as a leader in that moment.

Sympathy is another way to understand what another is feeling. Because it's more intellectual in nature, it has fewer risks of leading to emotional overwhelm; however, it may not be as effective at soothing others because it is more head-based than heart-based. I believe it's best to hone both skills. That way, if empathy isn't working so great in a certain situation, we can switch to sympathy and see if that works better (and vice versa).

Here are some tips and techniques I've seen work well for tuning into another's emotions:

1. Make sure you're in a relatively calm and emotionally quiet place internally.
2. Self-soothe as needed throughout the process of tuning into another.
3. Pay attention to the other person's breathing, posture, eyes, facial expressions, etc. Ask yourself, *If I were doing these things, how would I be feeling?*
4. Tune into your own gut feeling about what emotions this person is feeling. When you have some ideas, ask yourself, *Does that fit what I know about this person? Does it seem to ring true in this moment?*
5. Ask yourself, *What would I be feeling if I were in their shoes?* Then, check-in with your gut; *Does that seem to be what they're feeling?*

6. Test out your theories of how they're feeling by offering what you think they might be feeling. Try to have no attachment to being right. The point is to hone your skills and help them believe you're trying to see, understand, and respect their feelings.

SKILL TWO: THEIR EMOTIONS ARE ALWAYS VALID

Recall from working on our ability to navigate our own emotions that emotions are always valid. Anytime we start to judge emotions, we are heading in the direction of emotional repression. This is equally true when working with other people's emotions. We need to accept other people's feelings as perfectly valid. That doesn't mean that we necessarily agree with the story they're telling themselves that created the emotion. It only means that we accept and respect their emotions just as they are.

Recall also that emotions are unstoppable. That means that whether we like it or not, another person's emotions cannot be stopped. Judging their emotion will likely result in the person either emotionally shutting down with us or digging their heels in and pushing even harder for their emotions to be heard and justified. The more effective choice to maximize our influence is to accept another's emotions without question.

To be clear, we may or may not be OK with the way in which another person is expressing their emotions, but we accept the emotion itself as perfectly valid no matter what. In later sections, we will talk about how to set boundaries if someone's expression of their emotions is out of hand, but our focus right now is on completely accepting another's emotions.

I like to describe the practice of working with another's emotions as being akin to emotional Aikido. In case you're unfamiliar with it, the martial art of Aikido is about redirecting an attacker's energy so that it doesn't cause harm—rather than defending or counter-attacking. It is based on compassion for the attacker and concern for their well-being as well as our own. Whether we are talking about a physical fight or an emotional one, when we defend and counter-attack, the fight tends to escalate. If we avoid defending or counter-attacking and, instead, redirect another person's energy, the fight tends to de-escalate.

By accepting another's emotions carte blanche, we are taking our first step toward redirecting another's emotions rather than defending or counter-attacking. With no counterforce to work against, their emotion is more likely to dissipate. Soon after their emotion has been released, that person will be in a better place to have a reasonable, compassionate, and solution-focused conversation because the fight-or-flight response is no longer running them.

SKILL THREE: THEIR FEELINGS ARE THEIR RESPONSIBILITY, NOT OURS

Recall that the only person who can make us feel anything is ourselves. The same is true in reverse. Just like we are always responsible for our feelings, others are always responsible for theirs. This is an important understanding to have. It's liberating not to take responsibility for other people's feelings. It can also be scary.

When we get down to it, many of us have been conditioned to overly value trying to please others. If people we care about are displeased with us, we tend to be displeased with ourselves. If they are disappointed in us, we tend to be disappointed in ourselves. If they are joyous at our achievements, we tend to be joyous ourselves. This, in and of itself, can be perfectly fine. It's when we overly define our worth as a person on the opinions, thoughts, and feelings of others that it becomes problematic. That's how we lose track of who we really are. That's how we lose touch with mastering our own, unique Inner Game of Leadership.

Part of emotional and relational intelligence is learning to more clearly separate our identity and sense of self-worth from the perceptions, narratives, and feelings of others. Doing so requires that we know ourselves well, so we can internally check-in with who we really are when faced with judgments and emotions from others that may be distorted. Nowhere is that more important than in accepting that everyone creates their own feelings with their internal narratives. Thus, others' feelings are not our responsibility.

With that said, everyone has their emotional sensitivities (a.k.a. triggers). As a result, we can play a role in co-creating another's emotional reaction if we remain insensitive to their triggers. Thus, to maximize our influence as leaders, we need to be aware of each important person in our lives and develop some level of knowledge of what makes them tick so that we can better avoid, or at least show sensitivity to, their emotional vulnerabilities.

Compassion is key to maximizing our influence. It is when we show concern for another's well-being that they will likely feel most connected to us. It's in our desire to help another that others tend to feel most heard, valued, and respected for who they are. At the same time, our goal is to show concern for others without limiting ourselves or others by avoiding a necessary conversation.

For example, if we know someone is extra sensitive to criticism, it is more likely that the person can actually take in our feedback (instead of being overtaken by an emotional reaction) if we deliver that feedback in a way that demonstrates how we respect them and have a genuine desire to help them. So we might adjust the way in which we deliver that difficult conversation by softening our voice tone, making sure we're coming from a Heartset of discernment and not judgment, sincerely voicing that we have a lot of respect for them, and giving positive feedback before the negative.

Additionally, recognize that if others are blaming us for how they feel, they are playing the role of the victim on the Drama Paradigm, and they are perceiving us as the persecutor/villain. If we respond to their blame with our own anger, blame, or other emotional reaction, we have now stepped onto the Drama Paradigm ourselves and thus become an equal co-creator of unnecessary drama. Going back to the premise of emotional Aikido, if we respond with an emotional reaction of our own, we are counter-attacking rather than deflecting or redirecting.

To maximize our influence in this situation, we need to step into the Empowerment Paradigm by shifting into the role of a challenger/champion rather than a persecutor/villain. A challenger/champion shows respect and compassion for all while holding others accountable and championing them to step into their best self. For more details on how to shift our Mindset from that of a persecutor/villain to a challenger/champion, please refer to Chapter 5 – Advanced Mindset Skills.

SKILL FOUR: MINING OTHERS' EMOTIONS FOR USEFUL INFORMATION

When working with the emotions of others, it's very helpful to focus our attention on the useful information that their emotions are communicating to us. Do their emotions communicate joy? Achievement? Distress? Anxiety? Compassion? Composure? Reactivity?

Taking it one step further, the next thing to do is ask ourselves why that person might be feeling that way in this moment. To be more specific, if their emotions are signaling joy, why do we think that person feels joyful right now? Remember that we tend to feel joyful when things go the way we want them to go and disappointment when they don't. That doesn't necessarily mean that we anticipated the joyful event; it just means that when it happens, we feel joyful because it satisfies what we want in that moment.

Let's consider two different examples to illustrate this point. First, imagine coming home on a Wednesday evening after a long, hard day at work. You're feeling completely drained and all you want to do is relax for a bit, spend some quality time with your spouse, and go to bed early. When you arrive home, your spouse is in a high energy mood and really wants to go out that night to celebrate a recent promotion. You were aware of the promotion, but you were planning to go out to celebrate over the weekend. In that situation, you're likely to feel disappointed and maybe stressed because you don't want to let your partner down, but you're feeling drained.

Second, let's say you've worked hard all year going for that next, big promotion. As you are approaching your review session with your boss, you're feeling nervous because you know you didn't hit all your marks in spite of working very hard. In your opinion, you should still get that promotion, but you're not expecting your boss to agree because he tends to hold your feet to the fire over everything. As it turns out, the boss is more understanding than you were expecting, and you do get the promotion. You feel elated.

There are an infinite number of stories like these. Our goal in mining others' emotions for useful information is to get at the underlying cause of the emotions. That underlying cause will point us to some potentially valuable information about what makes this person tick, what is important to them, and what is not important to them. Their feelings are always indicators that reveal useful information to us if we just pay attention, look for them, and do a good enough job of managing our own emotions so we're not in a reactive state.

Here are some examples of how we can mine a person's feelings for the useful information they contain:

- Ask ourselves, *Given how they're feeling right now, what might have happened that triggered them to feel this way?* Then try out various scenarios in our mind and see which rings most true. For example:
    - What are some of the things that would make me feel this way? Perhaps that is also a trigger for this person?
    - Does their anger right now indicate that a boundary was crossed?
    - Or does this anger have nothing to do with work, and maybe there's something going on in their personal life?
    - Or maybe they're angry because they believe I'm not listening to them or valuing their contribution?
    - Or maybe it's something else entirely that they're angry about and it's coming out now?

149

- How might I be feeling if I were in their shoes? What would I be going through if I experienced what they experienced? What might those emotions be telling me about my own values and expectations?
- Once we have what we believe is a pretty solid theory, we can try compassionately voicing it to them, without showing attachment to our theory being right.
  - Then engage in a dialog to help them, and you, uncover what the useful information behind the emotion might be.
- We can also keep our theories to ourselves and just use it as information in how to best work with this person in this moment. We can try some emotional Aikido, perhaps compassionately redirecting their energy into a more positive direction.

SKILL FIVE: LEARNING HOW TO SOOTHE OTHERS

The better we are at soothing ourselves, the more equipped we will be at soothing others. The reasons for this are two-fold. First, the less reactive and more grounded we are, the more present we can be for someone else. Second, gaining mastery over soothing ourselves will teach us much of what we need to know about soothing others.

All four of the skills that have preceded this one will typically have the impact of soothing others. An unfortunate truth is that not many people, especially in work environments, pay much attention to the emotions of others. By developing our skills of being aware of others' emotions with increased empathy and sympathy, people will tend to feel more heard, valued, and respected in our presence – even without us saying anything.

Additionally, accepting their emotions without any judgment will also tend to impact them such that they are more accepting of their own emotions, and that will be soothing. Next, compassionately encouraging others to take responsibility for their own feelings while leading by example (by taking responsibility for our feelings) will also tend to have a soothing impact on others. And, finally, respectfully paying attention to the underlying causes of another's emotions will tend to lead them to believe that we have their best interests at heart—another soothing impact.

Another critical skill to soothing others is practicing conscious, heart-based listening. It is quite often the case that when we've really and fully heard someone through this practice, they will feel deeply soothed, and their emotions often dissipate entirely simply because they've been witnessed and respected by another human being.

Additionally, remember that people tend to mirror each other's emotions. If someone is angry with us, our natural inclination is usually to become angry back. However, this typically just results in escalation of conflict. The more effective and influential strategy is to practice emotional Aikido, redirecting the angry energy by simply not allowing that anger to trigger us. If we don't oppose the anger with anger of our own, the anger has nowhere to go, and it will likely dissipate. This is another example of how having some level of mastery over our own emotions is paramount to being able to effectively soothe and help others to better navigate their emotions.

Related to mirroring, a helpful technique that I've seen work well is to use our own self-soothing techniques. One such technique is taking a deep breath with the exhale longer than the inhale. When people are in the fight-or-flight response, breathing becomes shallow or they may even stop breathing altogether. This only puts our physiology into a deeper state of stress and exacerbates the fight-or-flight response. By emphasizing our calm breathing, the other person is more likely to calm their own breathing by unconsciously mirroring our breathing. In doing so, they will feel more soothed.

Finally, another powerful technique is to start directly mentoring and coaching others on how to do what you've learned to do to soothe yourself. Start with someone you have a high degree of trust in. Tell them the benefits that you've experienced by using these techniques, and offer them some possible ways they could potentially help themselves when they start getting overtaken by an emotional reaction. From there, you might even further enroll them in their own journey to master their Inner Game of Leadership.

Skill Six: Applying the 90-Second Rule to Others' Emotions

There are two key ways to utilize the 90-second rule in working with others' emotions. First, if any emotion another person is experiencing persists for more than 90 seconds, you know they are doing one or both of these two things: 1) repressing their emotion in some fashion; or 2) repeating the same story to themselves again and again, thereby re-triggering the emotion. The second key way in which to utilize the 90-second rule with others is to mentor them on what it means and how to practice it themselves.

Let's start by exploring how to make use of the knowledge that another is repressing their emotions. This is good for us to know because, remember, emotions are unstoppable. That emotion is eventually going to find a way out of that person, and emotions that have been repressed are more likely to eventually be expressed in a dysfunctional way.

So, what do we do with that information? First, if we notice passive-aggressive behavior from this person, we now have a sense of why that is happening. Second, we can likely help to prevent or at least reduce that passive-aggressive behavior in the future by revisiting our skills, which will tend to have a soothing effect on another.

Yet, for someone who's repressing their emotions, the skill that tends to be most effective in soothing them is practicing conscious, heart-based listening. When appropriate, look for opportunities to practice this more often with this person and see how they change toward you over time.

It's also helpful to know that you need to pick your battles. Of course, you can't afford to invest this much time with everyone. Choose the opportune moments with the right people. For example, a key subordinate that you rely on heavily is perhaps the person most worthy of your extra time to practice this.

Recall that when we're repeating the same story again and again to re-trigger an emotion, that story is typically coming from the Drama Paradigm. Therefore, another key thing to know is that if someone is repeating the same story to themselves, they are likely in a Mindset that has them trapped in the Drama Paradigm. If so, they are probably seeing themselves as a victim and someone or something else as the persecutor/villain.

The most important thing is for us to not join them in the Drama Paradigm; instead, stay firmly grounded in the Empowerment Paradigm. Next, it's typically most effective to help them release the emotion first with other techniques such as conscious, heart-based listening.

Then, we want to shift to coaching the person to understand that they are living in the Drama Paradigm. This, again, is something we need to be mindful of. It's not always warranted to shift into coaching someone who is stuck in the Drama Paradigm. We need to ask ourselves first:

- Just how important is this issue at this time? What is at stake here, and is it worth the effort now?
- Does coaching this person make sense given the nature of our relationship with them?
- What's the payoff for them, for me, and for the organization if we're successful in coaching this person to better navigate their own emotions?

SKILL SEVEN: HELPING OTHERS RELEASE THEIR EMOTIONS PRODUCTIVELY AND CONSTRUCTIVELY

There are three primary ways that we can help others to release their emotions productively and constructively. First, we must do our best to lead by example. Second, we must set boundaries with people when the way they're expressing their emotions is inappropriate. Finally, we can lean into directly mentoring and coaching others on how to improve their emotional intelligence.

First, the more we can embody our own emotional intelligence, the more inspired others will be to follow our lead. As we gain more mastery over our emotions, our presence will become stronger, we will become more influential, and people will be drawn to us more. People will also notice how we seem calmer and more grounded than the average person. They will wonder how we manage to do that, and they will want that for themselves. Most importantly, people will notice how much more effective we are as a leader. In short, the more we dive into mastering our own emotional intelligence, the more others around us will aspire to do the same.

The second key way in which we can help others, and help ourselves, in the context of emotions being released productively is to practice the skill of setting and enforcing boundaries when someone has crossed a line of inappropriate behavior. For instance, let's say a peer of ours tends to try to dump a lot of their work on us because they're constantly feeling stressed about their workload and they don't know how to push back on their boss when he asks for more than is realistic. Instead of pushing back on their boss, this person comes to you and asks you to pick up the slack. You think of yourself as a team player, and the first time this happens you have a little extra bandwidth, so you say yes.

But over time, a pattern develops, and it becomes clear that this person is abusing your desire to be a team player by dumping even more work on you while still taking credit for it. Your most important work is beginning to slip because you're now taking on too much, and it's not even work that your boss has asked you to do. It's time to communicate this problem, but how do you go about it?

First, know that you are worth it. Your time matters, and you have a right to take care of yourself. In fact, I believe it is imperative for us all to set appropriate boundaries. This benefits the organization as a whole, not just ourselves. It also benefits the person or people that we're setting the boundary with. In this example, for instance, communicating with this person that they've gone too far with their requests is a form of holding them accountable and implicitly communicating to them that they need to own their power and take care of themselves. Recall that this person is dumping on us because they feel stressed in response to not being comfortable pushing back on their boss who expects too much.

That's a difficult conversation that needs to happen, and we're actually enabling that person to avoid that conversation by not pushing back ourselves. It's a domino effect that works to no one's advantage, least of all the organization's. By enforcing our boundary, we are actually championing this person to step up and have that difficult conversation. That person may or may not end up having the difficult conversation with their boss, but that's not our problem. We've done our part for the organization by taking care of ourselves and not enabling this behavior.

When you come from the internal place of believing that you're worth it, knowing what's in the best interests of the organization, and recognizing that you're actually championing this person by holding them accountable, it will be much easier to find the words to say. And that's most likely all you need to do. Know that you may get some pushback as you are now upsetting what has become the status quo. Your job, however, is to stay the course and not allow this behavior to continue. The rest is up to the other people involved.

The final way that we can help others to express their emotions productively and constructively is to directly mentor and coach them on their emotional intelligence. The way we can best teach others is to utilize our own knowledge from practicing emotional intelligence inside ourselves. As we gain more mastery over these skills within ourselves, we will become clearer and clearer about how to coach and mentor others.

SKILL EIGHT: HELPING OTHERS CHOOSE THE EMOTIONS THEY SHOW

In helping others to better choose the emotions they show, we can really only do two things. First and foremost, we must lead by example by maximizing our own ability to consciously choose which emotions we show. In doing so, others will notice and may want to learn that themselves. The second thing we can do is to directly coach them on how to choose the emotions they show. For them to do that effectively, they will need a strong foundational practice of all prior seven skills. Thus, mentoring them in this arena is a longer endeavor. We need to choose wisely in whom we invest the time with in this way.

IN EVERY INTERACTION WITH EVERYONE, GIVE THEM AN EMOTIONAL GIFT

Imagine a world where everyone made a point of giving a small emotional gift to everyone else that they interacted with. Life is nothing more than a series of small moments strung together with the occasional BIG moment. What if we made a point of making everyone's small moments just a little bit better by giving them an emotional gift? How much better would people around us feel? Would they feel more connected to us and the environment? Would they be more likely to do their best work? Would they feel happier and more fulfilled? And while we might feel awkward at first when doing this, we will get used to it. It's just a matter of developing a new habit. Once that habit begins to take hold, we are likely to feel similar benefits ourselves.

Here's the best part: it doesn't have to be complicated or difficult. It can be as simple as these kinds of things:

- a warm smile
- giving our full presence with no screens or anything else distracting us
- asking about their family life

- listening intently and focusing only on hearing what they have to say
- making warm and supportive eye contact

It's fascinating how people tend to be more transactional in the workplace. In many organizational cultures, there seems to be an implicit assumption that we have to focus only on getting stuff done and we thereby tend to discount making the extra effort to be personal in how we interact with people. Remember: there's a crisis of disconnection at play in today's society and nowhere more so than in many work environments.

Chapter 10

Winning the Leadership Race with Your Heartset

THIS BOOK OPENED WITH an introduction that included a cliffhanger story about my 100 mph motorcycle crash that caused me to lose the championship lead halfway through the racing season. I ended up second in the championship when my number one goal in life was to win that championship. When the season ended and I came up short of my goal, I was devastated.

Soon after the season ended, my biggest rival (let's call him Sam), who'd won the championship, made a very unexpected announcement. He announced that he'd been diagnosed with leukemia and that he was retiring from racing. Of course, his life expectancy was, thus, very unclear. This unexpected turn of events led me to question what life was really all about. Was that championship *really* so important? Is life only about winning? If it is, that's not very fair because, by definition, not everyone can win. There's got to be more to life than just winning.

A part of me to this day still wishes I'd won that championship. In fact, I still have recurring dreams of returning to racing. These dreams have sometimes been so vivid that I've awoken with my heart pounding and the distinct feeling of the exhilaration of victory. For a few moments it all feels real again. As vivid and enticing as those dreams are, I also believe that the season championship couldn't have gone to a better competitor—one who would most likely never be able to race again.

One of the things that has most stuck with me from that race weekend when I crashed at 100 mph is how Sam stopped by and chatted with me while I was rebuilding my totaled bike. We had a friendly chat, and he commented on how I had a genuine smile on my face while I was going through that stressful day. It was a seemingly small moment and one that I've treasured ever since. In spite of my championship goals being very much at risk, I was able to be in a good mood, non-reactive, enjoying myself, and just focused on what I needed to do to reach my goals. In that stressful event, I was able to be relationship-focused and successfully rebuild my motorcycle at the same time. In fact, it was partly good relationships with other racers that made that possible as I had to borrow parts from other racers to have a complete bike to race that Sunday.

I chose to retire from racing after that season and have never again challenged for that kind of championship. Motorcycle road-racing at that level involves a lot of sacrifice. There were so many other things in my life I had postponed or even let fall apart to race, and I was at a point where I didn't see enough value in continuing to race in this way.

The experience of realizing there was so much more to life than winning changed my life forever. It led me to see that life is not just about results; it's also about relationships. It also helped me to appreciate just how much my success in racing hinged on the key relationships in my life. Some of those relationships included the ones I had with my staunchest competitors, including my friend Sam.

My experiences in that racing season led me to new beliefs about leadership and life. In essence, great leaders and great lives are created by finding the right balance between achievement and relationships. In fact, they have to go hand-in-hand to be able to achieve great things. We tend to get better results in life by being more relationship-focused and not just focused on winning. We tend to do our best work when we feel fulfilled and purposeful, working toward something that we believe has importance that extends beyond ourselves.

There's something about achievement that can be like an addictive drug. When we do something really well and get some notoriety, we tend to want more of that. Often a lot more of that. As a leader, it's easy to fall into the trap of forgetting how all the support from our relationships with others plays such a key role in getting to the top and being able to stay there. Many great leaders don't have staying power because they don't understand this quickly enough. They fall from grace with others because, essentially, their ego got the best of them, and they failed to stay in great relationship with those around them. The simple truth is that without strong relationships, we are no longer a leader.

Heartset is many things. If we were to net it out, optimizing our Heartset really comes down to this one essential question: Are we relating to ourselves and others in a way that inspires, motivates, and brings out the best in everyone? Our purpose has to include others and not just ourselves because we are always inextricably intertwined with others. If we choose to make our lives only about winning and believe we can get there on our own, then we're likely heading into a big, 100-mph crash.

Before wrapping up the Heartset section of the book, let's look again at our model of reactivity to illustrate what we're achieving as we optimize our Heartset. As we get better and better at Heartset, we will re-set our baseline such that we are operating at the level of an emotional high more and more often. We will work through and process our emotions more quickly, thus allowing ourselves to be more high-functioning more of the time. We will also better relate to others and tend to impact them to do more of their best work – this is where the multiplier effect on others becomes more evident. When we improved our Mindset, we recalibrated our reactions to more closely match the reality of our circumstances. Now, as we improve our Heartset, we will experience a shift to operating from a higher functioning zone more often.

In the updated illustration of the model of reactivity (see figure 10.1), we can see in the solid dark line how we are now operating at a higher level.

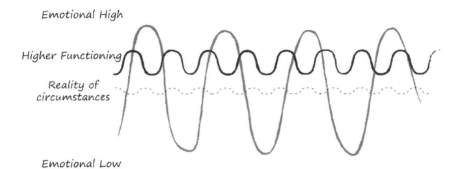

Figure 10.1 – Reactivity Model with Improved Heartset

This leads us into the next section of the book, which is about putting all of this into practice with specific skills for increasing influence and putting our improved Mindset and Heartset to use, day in and day out. This next section is where the motorcycle racing rubber meets the road!

PART 4

Putting It into Practice

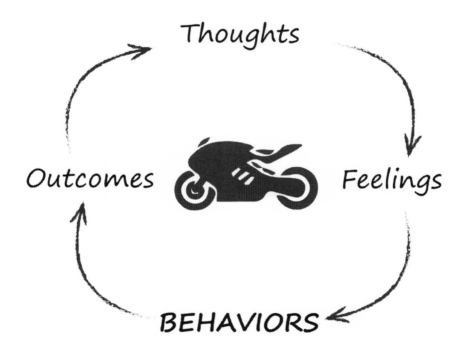

Chapter 11

Practice Does Not Make You Perfect, But It Does Make You Better

WHEN I FIRST BEGAN to race motorcycles, one of my weakest points as a competitor was the start of the race. It seemed like no matter what I did, I would get off the starting line quite slowly, and other racers would pass me right away. Since I was already a very good racer in other ways, I would then have to work my way back past many of these racers who had passed me at the starting line.

I recognized right away that my starting technique was something I needed to get better at if I wanted to win. I set out to analyze the best starting technique and quickly realized that the skills involved boil down to these three things:

1. Holding the clutch in, transmission in first gear, and then redlining (maximum RPM) the motor while waiting for the green flag (signifying the start of the race) to drop
2. Timing my reaction to the green flag to be as quick as possible, yet not so fast that I jump the start and get penalized
3. Letting the clutch out at just the right rate to maximize acceleration. Let it out too slowly and acceleration is lost. Let it out too quickly and the motorcycle will wheelie and acceleration is lost.

These starting skills are a fine balancing act to get just right. It was tedious to me to practice these skills, but I forced myself to practice religiously. Eventually, I became one of the better starters in my racing class, and my starting technique was no longer a weakness. But practice does not make perfect...

A few months into my second year of road-racing, I had earned the right to be gridded on the front row for the very first time. This meant no racers were in front of me at the starting line. At the same time, this also meant that there were more than 50 racers behind me at the start. Any significant mistake could mean catastrophe, not just in terms of a bad start but also in terms of physical danger for me and everyone else.

After we did our sighting lap, I pulled up to the starting line alongside the other racers gridded on the front row and put my front wheel on my mark. The starter was still showing the number 3 sign, indicating we had a few minutes before the actual start of the race while everyone was still getting situated on the grid. Since we had a few minutes, and it was a hot day where I didn't want to risk my clutch overheating, I put the motorcycle into neutral and left the engine idling.

The race starter goes through a starting sequence on every race so that all the racers know exactly what to expect. The next sign he showed was the number 2, indicating we were getting closer to the green flag. At that point, I put my helmet visor down and began to go through my mental preparation for the start of the race – going inward in my thinking and beginning to shut out everything else. I wanted to focus on what mattered most and not be distracted.

A minute or so later, the starter showed the number one sign, meaning that the race would begin within one minute or less. This is the point where everyone's adrenaline really starts to spike. (My adrenaline is spiking now just writing about it!) And then, there's something about hearing **everyone's** bike motor go up to redline while waiting for the green flag that amps up the adrenaline that much more. The starter then turned the one sign sideways, indicating he would drop the green flag sometime within the next five seconds. A second or two after he turned the one sideways, I panicked for a split second as I realized my bike was still in neutral! I quickly put the bike in gear, mentally breathing a sigh of relief as I averted that potentially huge disaster. About a second later, the green flag dropped and the race was off!

In spite of my mistake, I got a really good start and exited the first corner in second place. Before the finish of that first lap, I passed into the lead of the race and later took the checkered flag with an exciting race victory. There's something about the feeling of winning a motorcycle race that sticks with you forever, and this one certainly felt sweet.

The outcome could have been very different. I could have mentally beat myself up after that rookie mistake on the starting line. If I had expected myself to be perfect, that's what I would have done. Then, in beating myself up, I would have distracted myself during the race with my negative self-talk and undermined my performance. But I didn't expect myself to be perfect. Partly because I'd practiced so much, I was able to immediately let that mistake go and then be present to exactly what I needed to do next to get the job done.

Practice will never make us perfect, but consistent and mindful practice will make us a whole lot better. Not only will it make us better day-in and day-out, it will also greatly enhance our ability to recover quickly when we do make a mistake. That's why mastering our Inner Game of Leadership is not about being perfect. It's about being committed to our growth, staying in the game even when it's hard, and especially staying in the game on our bad days and bad moments.

One of the beauties of mastering our Inner Game of Leadership is that we will never be fully done. We will never arrive at any state of perfection. If we ever start to think that we should be perfect, we're setting ourselves up for a fall. If ever we start to think that we are actually perfect, we're setting ourselves up for an even bigger fall. It's a paradox, but the more we mindfully practice and accept that we will make mistakes sometimes – maybe even total rookie mistakes when we're no longer a rookie – the less likely we are to make those mistakes in the first place and the more able we are to quickly recover when things do go wrong.

The putting-it-into-practice section of this book is about improving our mastery over our Inner Game of Leadership with mindful and practical application of our improved Mindset and Heartset. It's also about deepening our commitment to our growth and learning. It's definitely about results too – because the best results tend to be created when we practice mindfully, focus on our growth and learning, and give ourselves the freedom that can only come from knowing that we will treat ourselves exquisitely well no matter what.

Chapter 12

Applying Your Mindset and Heartset Skills in a VUCA World

THIS CHAPTER IS MEANT to provide you with some key ways to practically put your improved Mindset and Heartset into action in real-world situations. I believe you will find these tips to be practical, actionable, and on-point with some of the leadership challenges you regularly face.

It will be helpful for you to think of this chapter as your playbook for leading in a VUCA world. After reading this chapter and putting some of these tips into action, you may want to deepen your learning by imagining – and putting into practice – all the many other ways in which you can put your improved Inner Game of Leadership to work. In fact, to get the most out of this book, I suggest that you write your own leadership playbook that includes scenarios you are commonly faced with and how you can best apply your improved Inner Game of Leadership to those scenarios.

MAKING DIFFICULT DECISIONS IN A VUCA WORLD

In today's fast-paced, ever-changing world, we need to get more comfortable making decisions with many competing priorities and incomplete, imperfect information. Recall from Chapter 7 that in a

VUCA world, emotion-based decision-making can actually be more effective than taking a rational approach.

Malcolm Gladwell's wonderful book *Blink* talks about how, with enough experience, our brains can do what psychologists call thin-slicing. With thin-slicing, our brains automatically filter decisions down to the very few factors that matter, make a very good decision based on those key factors, and then communicate that decision to us in the form of our intuition. In many cases, that thin-sliced intuition produces a better decision than rational thought. The quality of a thin-sliced decision is especially likely to be better when the decision has VUCA characteristics.

So, what do you do when you have a tough decision to make and no clear answer? First, breathe. Then, feel what it's like to be in your body. Take a walk if you can. Feel your feet beneath you. Not feeling it yet? Take some more deep and slow breaths, focusing on the physical sensation of breathing. Feel your chest and lungs fill as you take a deep breath, and then feel the relaxation as you exhale, letting your mind and body release. Now that you've successfully pulled your analytical mind away from the problem at hand for a few minutes, your heart and intuition will likely have something to "tell" you. In this calm and clear place, what feels right? What's your gut "telling" you?

You may be surprised at the increased clarity that can result from mindfully slowing down and tuning in to your intuition. Your intuition may know how to proceed more quickly and accurately than your analytical mind, if you can set aside your analytical mind for a few minutes and just let your intuition flow.

One risk of following our intuition is that it may encourage us to make decisions that are based in unconscious biases. The good news is, the more we master our Inner Game of Leadership, the better equipped we are to overcome any unconscious biases we may be carrying, as we will see in the next section.

Questions for reflection:

- How consistent is your meditation practice? The more consistent you are with your practice, the more in touch with your intuition you are likely to be.
- Do you have a tendency to over-analyze? What would it be like to trust your gut more often?
- Are you overly worried about making the wrong decision?
- How much information is enough information to make this decision?

OVERCOMING OUR UNCONSCIOUS BIASES

One of the benefits that has stemmed from the difficult events of 2020 is that diversity, equity, and inclusion seem to have reached a critical tipping point. I'm not sure these issues have ever been more top of mind or top of heart in the world than they are now.

In my view, there is no neutral ground on anything. That means either we're thinking, feeling, and behaving in a way that makes us a part of the solution, or we are a part of the problem. Nowhere is that more true than on issues of social justice. So, let's look at how mastering our Inner Game of Leadership will help us to be a part of the solution.

First and foremost, we need to accept that we all carry some level of implicit and unconscious bias. This, in part, goes back to our childhood experiences, and how we internalized those experiences. However good our childhood might have been, we inevitably end up internalizing some distorted beliefs and emotional associations that hinder us as adults. As we have seen, uncovering our unconscious beliefs and replacing them with more empowering, reasonable, and fair-minded beliefs is a core requirement for mastering our Inner Game of Leadership. As such, the work of mastering Our Inner Game of Leadership will serve us well in unlearning our implicit biases.

Here are some of the key ways in which we can apply the work we're already doing to master our Inner Game of Leadership to overcoming our unconscious biases:

1. How we do anything is how we do everything

Recall from Chapter 4 that how we do anything is how we do everything. This means any thoughts, feelings, or behaviors we have are likely to be indicators of a pattern in our Inner Game of Leadership and not just a one-off based on our current circumstances. So, as we become more conscious of our automatic thoughts, feelings, and behaviors we have to assume that these are habitual. Thus, we need to take a systematic, critical, and compassionate look at ourselves as we work toward shedding any implicit biases so that we can be a part of the social justice solution. One helpful way to deepen our understanding of our own implicit biases is to take an implicit association test. One that I know works well is the Harvard Implicit Association Test.

2. Meditation

As you may recall from Chapter 4, meditation is one of the foundational elements of mastering our Inner Game of Leadership. A consistent passive meditation practice will develop our minds to have more capacity for compassion and be less reactive, which will enable us to be more conscious in how we respond to any given situation. Once we have established this strong foundation, we can begin to practice active meditation in order to cultivate mindful responses to any situation where social justice issues are at play. Our meditation practice will enable us to more easily watch our thoughts, feelings, and actions and spot any problems that may hinder our ability to walk the talk of social justice. Once you've advanced far enough in your meditation practice, begin to use it to uncover any implicit biases you are carrying. The next step after that is to use your active meditation practice to "catch yourself in the act" of thinking, feeling, or behaving in an unfairly biased way and make a different choice in the moment to be fair and socially just.

3. Self-talk

One of the first places to look to uncover your implicit biases is your inner dialog. Recall that as much as 95% of our thoughts are repetitive, and the vast majority of our thoughts are unconscious and automatic. This system within our brains that makes thoughts habitual and pushes them into our subconscious as they become automatic serves us well in many contexts. At the same time, this system is problematic when it comes to overcoming our unconscious biases. In order to overcome our unconscious biases, we must first become aware of them. To do that, we must expand the monitoring of our inner dialog to focus on self-talk that might get in the way of our ability to be fair with all human beings. Start monitoring your self-talk for any thoughts that are biased. Once you become more aware of those thoughts, write them down and come up with some fair-minded thoughts to replace them. If you've done an implicit association test, those results will give you some ideas of what kinds of biased thoughts you might be having. Use that as a starting point to kick off your exploration of your inner dialog on issues of social justice.

4. You are the product of the people you are closest to

The people we choose to spend the most time with and hold closest in our lives have an outsized effect on our attitudes, beliefs, and unconscious biases. If we are surrounded by people who hold unconscious biases against any group of people, we are more likely to develop and/or reinforce those same biases. Also, if the people we spend the most time with all come from a similar socio-economic, racial, gender, and sexual preference as we do, it will be harder for us to understand and fairly treat others who are different from us. In order to be a part of the solution for social justice issues, we need to take it upon ourselves to proactively create and sustain relationships with diverse sets of people. We also need to be mindful of the people we are closest to and cultivate as many relationships as possible with people who practice equal treatment for all and are diligent in their approach to improving their own implicit biases.

Questions for reflection:

- To what extent are you working diligently toward overcoming your unconscious biases?
- To what extent are you walking the talk of social justice in your life and work? How do you know if you are or aren't walking the talk?
- Are you consciously surrounding yourself with people from diverse backgrounds?
- How are you working to become more consciously aware of your implicit biases? What are you proactively doing to overcome your unconscious biases?

THE DELICATE BALANCE BETWEEN LEADING AND STILL BEING A PART OF THE TEAM

The very definition of leadership requires a leader to stand apart from the crowd. If we're simply doing the same thing everyone else is doing, we're not leading at all. We're following.

Yet we've all known leaders that strayed too far from the beliefs of their constituents or appeared to put on airs of being superior to the group and, in so doing, lost influence. While they might hold on to the title associated with being a leader for some time, their true influence is greatly diminished because they're no longer meeting people where they're at.

To be a great leader, we must be respected and seen as a visionary. We must also be seen as someone who's willing to risk social rejection for the sake of taking the group in a better direction. But at the same time, we must be seen as a part of the group. If not, we risk losing too many people and appearing to be a solitary eccentric who is to be ignored rather than a great visionary who is to be followed.

Thus, one of the great paradoxes of leadership is being able to be ahead of the crowd, consistently doing things differently than the herd, while also still being seen as a part of the group we're leading.

Here are three keys to doing just that:

1. Meet people where they're at and be influenced by them.

As an unshakeable leader who is interested in maximizing our influence, we must be vigilant in taking responsibility for meeting people where they're at rather than expecting them to come to us. If people don't understand our position, that's our fault, and we need to adjust how we're speaking so that they do. If people aren't paying attention to what we have to say, that's also our fault. We need to learn how to speak our truth from our heart, solidly grounded in the purity of our truth while also being receptive to everyone else's opinion and not making them feel wrong. When we speak from that place, people will have a much harder time ignoring us. We also need to really listen to others and allow ourselves to be influenced by them while still holding true to our core beliefs and what we're aiming for as leaders.

2. Be a chameleon, without being disingenuous.

Great leaders know that they must be able to find common ground with as many people as possible. This makes us relatable and helps others around us to feel seen, heard and respected. This in turn engenders trust, which makes others more likely to be genuinely influenced by us.

Like many things in leadership, this is a fine line. Take being a chameleon too far, and we risk being perceived as blowing with the wind and not having any solid beliefs of our own. But go too far the other direction and we start coming across as a lone dictator. We can, perhaps, get others to comply by the authority of our position, but they're not really bought in and may silently sabotage our efforts through lack of engagement – or worse.

3. Value relationships more than the deadline.

Unshakeable leaders value relationships more than the currently imminent deadline. We know that each deadline will come and go, but if we're doing our job right as a leader, most of our constituents will **not** come and go. That's right: deadlines are expendable, and our people aren't.

This again is a balancing act. Of course deadlines matter. Without clear deadlines, projects would be far more likely to take longer than they should. A great deadline stretches people to achieve more than they have ever done before. A great deadline also is realistic enough that it can be achieved.

But a great deadline is rarely more important than the great people we've got on our team. And again, if we're doing our job right as a leader, everyone on our team is great and heading into even greater territory.

Questions for reflection:

- What more can you do to meet people where they're at?
- How willing are you to adjust your style to better match the style of others?
- How often do you demonstrate in your behavior that your people matter more than the immediate deadline?

DEEPENING OUR PROFESSIONAL RELATIONSHIPS BY GETTING PERSONAL

Unshakeable leaders play a catalyzing role in creating and generating deeper connections between people. We know that we all have a fundamental need for connection as human beings and that we are all happier and more productive when we are more connected to others. Thus, we take the time to really get to know our colleagues, especially about things that have nothing to do with work.

We make a point of talking with people even when we don't have a professional reason to reach out and especially when we don't need anything at all from them. We ask about personal lives. In short, we show them that we really care, and we mean it. One of the more effective ways to practice this is to make a point of asking open-ended questions, and then practice conscious, heart-based listening. Listening in this way is a powerful tool for building deeper connection.

Feel like you've already got a good enough handle on creating strong connections through showing genuine interest and empathy for others? Perhaps it's time to try a more advanced way of building connection. Ask a bolder question that people rarely ask, such as, "What are you passionate about?" or "What made you smile today?" You may get some double-takes after asking such a bold question. And, many leaders are very pleasantly surprised at the more authentic answers and the more genuine connection these questions create than the rote question "How are you?" or "How's it going?"

Questions for reflection:

- How often do you stop by, or call, just to say hello to someone at work?
- Do you share personal things about yourself that aren't obvious?
- Do you ask personal questions of others and have genuine interest in them as a person?
- How often do you consciously choose to get curious about someone, ask open-ended questions, and then just listen to them?

It's Lonely at the Top – and What to Do About It

When I led a motorcycle race for the first time, it was a little eerie because I no longer had anyone else to follow. For the first time ever, I was setting the pace for an entire field of racers, and it felt a bit lonely to be honest. I wouldn't trade that amazing feeling of leading a race for anything, but I wasn't expecting the lonely part of it.

The same is true in leadership. The higher we progress in our organization, the lonelier it gets. Many leaders don't foresee this challenge because they're so focused on reaching their goals. We need to be as proactive as possible in preparing ourselves for the fact that it's lonely at the top because once we're in the situation it may be too late to do much about it.

By definition, as we rise closer and closer to the highest position in the organization, our peer group gets smaller and smaller. We also tend to feel less and less like we can truly and completely trust anyone in our organization. But to thrive as unshakeable leaders, we need trusted confidantes that have walked a mile in our shoes and people we can openly discuss anything and everything with. In short, we need strong connections with others. If we don't have that, the quality of our decision-making will decrease, our effectiveness as leaders will decrease, and our stress levels will increase.

That's why we need to cultivate relationships with trusted peers who are not in our organization. That's also why we need to cultivate relationships with independent mentors, coaches, and guides who can help us. Because when we're in the senior level role, we need to be at our best, but the loneliness of being at or near the top of the organizational hierarchy will often undermine our ability to succeed. Proactively investing in quality, outside peer groups and trusted mentors and coaches will pay big dividends in your career, success, and fulfillment.

Questions for reflection:

- How strong of a network of peers outside your office do you have?
- Do you have mentors outside the company you can turn to that you completely trust?
- How often do you seek counsel from trusted advisors and coaches?
- Are you relying too heavily on people inside the organization?
- How can you shift to more external mentor, coach, and peer support for yourself?

DON'T BE ADDICTED TO LEADERSHIP BY HEROISM

A common problem many leaders face is the tendency to reward heroes in the organization or even lead by being a hero.

While leaders may state otherwise, too often the implicit rewards of an organizational culture heavily favor heroism. Things like who gets the big promotion, who garners the most influence, who has the executive's ear, and who is treated like they walk on water are what drive behavior to a large degree.

Going the extra mile when it's needed is great. Rising to the occasion of a challenging deadline is good behavior. It's when this starts to become the norm that problems arise.

Why is this a problem?

1. Being a hero is addictive.

There's a strong high that can come from saving the day. The accolades, sense of accomplishment, and feeling "special" is great. But this too often leads to the ultimately self-defeating cycle of an addict "jonesing" for their next score of adoration – but it's never as good as the first time. Moreover, when the best rewards come to those who are consistently heroic, it typically creates an environment where everyone wants to be a hero.

2. Not everyone can be a hero.

The very definition of a hero means that it's an elite position that only a few can live into. Cultures that overly reward heroic behavior operate on the implicit assumption that everyone should aspire to be a hero. Yet, by definition, if everyone is a hero, then no one is. This leads to only the very elite getting the lion's share of attention and rewards and everyone else feeling like they can't measure up to an impossible standard. This is demoralizing to the multitude of have-nots, especially since the bulk of the work that must get done in any sizable organization lies in the hands of the masses.

3. Heroes hide deeper problems.

Hero cultures tend to be so enamored with heroic behavior – being wicked smart and working insane hours – that they don't give enough consideration to *why* there is so often a need for heroic behavior. Much of the time, there are some serious underlying issues like processes that are broken or can't scale or don't exist, under-trained staff, poor product quality, poor customer service, etc.

4. Heroes inevitably create burnout.

The addiction to being a hero is no different than any other addiction; while it may "light up" the pleasure centers of our brains in the short term, it's ultimately more damaging than it is helpful.

No matter how brilliant, hard-working, and heroic an employee might be, no human being can keep up this kind of driving-themselves-to-the-bone pace forever. Almost without fail, the perennial hero realizes they have to slow down. They may develop stress-related illnesses, or experience disastrous effects on their personal lives, or worse – work themselves to death. All the while believing that they're so special that these inevitable human truths don't apply to them.

5. Heroes spawn information hoarding and turf-building.

A culture that overly rewards heroism often leads to hiding of information as well as protecting and building one's "turf." While heroism doesn't require this behavior, too many people end up trying to put themselves in a position to be a hero by keeping information to themselves and building/protecting their territories in an overly self-serving way.

6. Heroes disempower and don't scale.

Heroes often end up becoming addicted to being a hero to a large extent because the implicit rewards of the company culture feed their heroism addiction. This causes many heroes to spend too much of their time on saving the day and not enough time on transferring knowledge and skills to others so that their brilliance can scale far beyond a single individual.

The true power and best profitability of any sizable organization lies in the strength of the masses and not in any one individual.

Questions for reflection:

- Are you too much of a hero? How can you shift yourself from the rescuer/hero Mindset to the coach/mentor Mindset?
- Is your organization too much of a hero culture? How can you help to shift your culture away from the rescuer/hero mindset and toward the Coach/Mentor Mindset?
- In what ways might you be implicitly rewarding hero behavior with your leadership style and leadership choices?

HOW TO NAVIGATE OFFICE POLITICS

One common challenge that nearly every leader faces is office politics. Leaders often have a distaste for office politics, but the fact is that in any organization with two or more people, politics will almost certainly come into play. Thus, perhaps the most important lesson to learn about office politics is that they are pretty much unavoidable.

We tend to have a distaste for office politics because it smacks of underhanded backstabbing, or at least below-board, back-room discussions where decisions are being made in an elitist manner. Further, it rings of people saying one thing to our faces, and then doing or saying something else behind our backs. Finally, it suggests that some people are "in" and others are "out."

As a result of the inherent distaste we leaders may have for office politics, we tend to treat it in one of the following three dysfunctional ways:

1. Burying our heads in the sand
2. Utilizing politics primarily for our own personal gain because we assume that's the only way to get ahead

3. Trying to deal with politics as best as we can, but our distaste for it gets in the way of really engaging with it in a productive way

What I often say to leaders I coach is this: ignore office politics at your own and your team's peril. What this means is you, and those who work for you, can't avoid being impacted by office politics. If you're not consciously and actively working on your relationships with key stakeholders (i.e. office politics), your likelihood of being blindsided and/or excluded from important decision-making increases dramatically. Is that really the best way to serve your team and the greater good of the organization? Not playing the "game" of office politics does not preclude you from being impacted by the game. If anything, trying to stay out of the game only increases the odds that you and your team will be negatively impacted by it.

Human beings are wired to be social and connect with each other emotionally. We will always have the tendency to connect more deeply with (and therefore tend to be more influenced by) those we know better, those we spend more time with, and those we trust more as a result of a broader range of shared experiences, activities, and communication. The sooner we accept the practical inevitability of office politics and proactively, and with good conscience, work with the office politics of our organization, the better.

If you continue to allow yourself to feel a distaste for office politics, that distaste will impede your ability to work effectively within the system. It will show up in your emotional tone with others as you participate in "political" activities. That emotional tone will then undermine what you're trying to accomplish, which is simply improving your relationships with key stakeholders in your organization to maximize your effectiveness as leaders.

Rather than lamenting the presence of politics in their organizations, unshakeable leaders know they are better served by consciously working with the politics of their organization. From that perspective, our way of approaching politics changes significantly.

Rather than asking ourselves, *Why do I have to deal with politics,* we accept its presence and, instead, ask ourselves questions like: *How can I work within the organizational politics in a way that suits my integrity and best serves the organization?* From there, we can extend our inner dialog to include questions like:

- Who are the most influential people in the organization? How can I build better relationships with those people?
- Who is working the political landscape well? What can I learn from them?
- Who is working politics with integrity and for the greater good of the organization? What can I learn from them?
- Who seems largely out for themselves? How can I best work with those people?
- Who is burying their head in the sand about politics? How do I better work with them?
- Who finds politics a distasteful "necessity" to get ahead in life? How do I influence them to see it in a more productive way for the greater good of the organization?

Another key question to consider is this: are we working the political system of our organization in a way that is intended to drive better outcomes for everyone, or are we mostly just out for ourselves? This is a time when we need to apply our introspection and self-honesty skills that were introduced in Chapter 4. If that introspection reveals that we're mostly just out for ourselves, then it's time to consider whether or not that really constitutes doing our job to the best of our ability. People will recognize that we're mostly out for ourselves. As a result, they will treat us more transactionally, trust us less, and are unlikely to do their best work for us.

Recall that the only way to scale ourselves as leaders is through our influence. If we are mostly out for ourselves, we're undermining our influence. And on a personal level, overly serving ourselves will nearly always come back to bite us in the end. Being out of integrity in this way tends to lead to burnout, addiction, and depression. If you self-identify as someone who is overly looking out for yourself, please know that many of the Mindset and Heartset skills in this book are likely to shift that tendency to be more compassionate. Your job is to recognize the issue within yourself first and then practice these skills diligently.

Organizations should strive to be true meritocracies and be as transparent as reasonably possible. At the same time, I know from decades of experience working with executives, teams, and organizations that if you choose to ignore politics, you are putting yourself and your team in peril. Office politics are actually neutral and a normal facet of human behavior. It really comes down to how you use politics. Are you using politics to do your very best to serve the greater good of the organization? Or are you using office politics for more nefarious purposes?

We can't control others, make them stop playing politics, or force them to play it in the way we want them to. Instead, we can focus on working with politics in a constructive way. This is where we can draw on our inner Heartset skills to manage any emotional reaction we may have to office politics.

Questions for reflection:

- What assumptions and automatic negative thoughts do we have about politics?
- How can we shift those automatic thoughts in order to work with politics in a productive way?
- How can we be grateful for office politics? What good does it serve?
- Are we stuck in a victim Mindset in regards to politics? If so, how can we shift into a co-creator Mindset?

KNOW THE KEY INFLUENCERS IN YOUR ORGANIZATION

To maximize your influence in your organization, one of your key skills needs to be maximizing your influence with the biggest influencers in the organization. In fact, there is perhaps no greater multiplier effect on your unshakeable influence than becoming highly influential amongst the most influential people.

The highest influence people are the people who play key roles in major decisions and whose opinions and thoughts are highly sought after in the organization. These people may have relatively senior titles and positions on the organizational chart, or they may not. Some people, through their deep domain expertise and/or relationship focused leadership style, will have significantly more influence than their title would seem to suggest. And sometimes the opposite happens. Sometimes someone with a very senior title and high position in the organizational hierarchy has less influence than you would expect because they're not great at their jobs and/or are not relationship-focused, inspirational leaders.

Maximum influence favors the well-prepared and frowns on the under-prepared. It's critical for us to be conscious in our approach to building and strengthening relationships that increase our influence. Many leaders are too haphazard in their approach to this, and it undermines their unshakeable influence. So, how do we become more mindful in our approach?

The first thing we want to do is to create a living document where we **write down** who the biggest influencers are in our organization. The criteria for identifying the most influential people include:

- Their position on the organizational chart
- Their level of influence
  - Are they sought-after experts?
  - When they speak, do people stop, turn their heads, and listen?
  - Do others seem to enjoy being around them?

- Are they skilled at relationships and leadership? Do they inspire and motivate people with their presence?
- Do they offer useful insight in most every conversation?
- Are they sought out by other highly influential people?

Additionally, we want to give more attention to people who are key stakeholders in projects we are responsible for delivering on in the next 12-18 months. If they're not key stakeholders yet they're highly influential, it may still be useful to proactively cultivate or deepen a relationship with them, but it probably needs to be lower on your priority list.

Once we've identified the key influencers, we want to identify and write down their top 2-3 business priorities for the next 12-18 months. Then, for each key influencer, identify the top 2-3 things we know makes them tick personally. Writing all this down will force us to get clearer on our answers to these questions. It will also enable us to track the information better because we simply cannot track all of it in our minds. We also need to revisit the information in this document every so often because our priorities will change over time, the key influencers will change over time, and our knowledge of the key influencers will increase over time.

When it comes to identifying the top 2-3 business priorities for another person, if you're not sure, simply ask them. The leaders I work with nearly always report that people are happy to answer this question when asked. You can frame it right up front as an alignment conversation to find ways to best support each other's success. Of course, you want to be ready to share your top 2-3 business priorities too. Most people welcome this kind of conversation.

Identifying the top 2-3 things that make each influencer "tick" is trickier. In most relationships, it is not something we would feel appropriate to ask directly. You will need to develop this with intuition, insight, and trial and error over time. Here are some questions you can ask yourself:

- What makes them happy?
- What makes them angry?
- What motivates them to do their best work?

For example, some people's biggest motivation might come from public praise. For others, what might motivate the most is the satisfaction of rising to the occasion of a big challenge and then getting a pat on the back in private. Other people might be relatively controlling and have a tendency to micro-manage or get lost in the weeds.

Tracking things in their personal life that you can discuss with them is also helpful, such as details about their family, their hobbies, and anything that they're passionate about. The idea is to get familiar with what they value and what they don't. This will make it easier for you to deepen relationships, find common ground, and make it a win-win for them to support you and us to support them.

This exercise will do a number of things for you. First, it will give you better visibility into the biggest strategic priorities of the entire organization by uncovering what each executive's biggest priorities are. Second, it will give you deeper insight into where the true power of the organization lies. Third, it will provide you with vital information necessary for framing your initiatives in terms that will most resonate with others and will most help them to be successful. People generally want to help others. The problem is everyone is super busy. If we frame things to them in the terms that they most care about, we have a better chance of getting their buy-in to support us.

Fourth, this exercise will give you a much better sense for what makes each leader tick on a personal level, and that can only be helpful in learning how to best influence them. Fifth, this will give you a stronger feel for what it takes to succeed in your company. Because you've targeted only the most influential people, this exercise has the helpful benefit of giving you a feel for the DNA of a successful leader at this organization. You might discover that your default leadership style is a good fit for the type of leader that tends to be successful here. Or, conversely, you might discover that your default leadership style is not a good fit for what is typically most successful here. Either way, that knowledge can only help you.

Finally, all of this information gives you a much more thorough understanding for how to find win-win scenarios for collaborating with these most influential people and their teams. And that's really the main point of this exercise, to help you increase your influence by becoming more influential amongst the most influential people in your company.

To embrace this exercise, we must accept that we are completely dependent on others to get things done. With that in mind we, of course, need to have the strongest possible relationships with the biggest influencers in the organization. Using this exercise may feel like manipulation but, as I said earlier, we're all manipulating each other all the time. We just need to be focused on the greater good—not out for ourselves.

Questions for reflection:

- How does this exercise help me, my team, and the organization?
- Given what I now know about each key influencer, how can I best meet them where they're at? How can I create a win-win with each key influencer?
- How can I apply my relational Heartset skills to navigate these relationships and maximize my influence?
- How can I apply conscious, heart-based listening to my interactions with these key influencers?

GET FEEDBACK AS OFTEN AS POSSIBLE

No matter how self-aware we may become, we will always have blind spots and areas for improvement that others can see more clearly than we can. Leaders who learn to regularly solicit and embrace candid feedback from others give themselves a huge competitive advantage in the leadership race of the 21st century. In soliciting and receiving feedback on a regular basis, we leaders can quickly recalibrate our experience of ourselves (our inner game) with how others perceive us. The problem is: very few leaders know how to solicit and receive feedback well. As a result, many leaders procrastinate when it comes to soliciting and receiving feedback. Then, if they do ever get around to getting feedback from others, it's often solicited poorly and received poorly.

As a personal example of the struggle to relate to feedback in a constructive way, within the last few years I invested time and money with a great video production company to film me at some of my speaking gigs, shoot some interview footage, and put together a compelling "speaker reel" so that prospective clients and meeting organizers could get a solid impression of me before meeting me personally. This was a significant investment and a clear opportunity to grow my business. I definitely felt like there was a lot at stake with getting this video production "right."

When a final cut of the video was made available for me to view, I felt very excited to see it. But as soon as I started watching it, I began to criticize myself for all the things I thought I was doing wrong. I felt demoralized because I'd put so much time and resources into the project, and I was very disappointed with what I saw. I was in such **self-judgment** about it that I could barely get myself to even finish watching the four-minute video. I did end up watching the entire thing, but it was hard.

Soon after watching the video that first time, I internally paused and made a conscious choice to say to myself, *That was my reaction this time. I don't have to repeat that reaction the next time I watch it. I have a conscious choice in how I react to seeing myself on video.* I gave myself a couple of days and then watched it again. This time I watched it with consciously-created curiosity and self-compassion. As a result, I had a very different experience. I could see how impactful this person was being (this person who also happened to be me) because I was more objective and compassionate in the way I was viewing it.

Not only could I now see things about myself that I didn't see before, the experience actually turned out to be transformative. I was able to recognize my gifts more clearly. And here's the kicker: when the video was complete, it was incredibly well-received by clients, prospects, and colleagues. It was a smashing success in a way that I simply could not see when I first viewed it because I was too caught up in my own self-criticism.

It is only when we're on camera that we have an opportunity to learn about ourselves in this way – seeing ourselves exactly as others see us. Being filmed is a huge gift, and many people rarely have that opportunity. Those who do often become overly critical of themselves and, thus, stop the flow of their learning. From that fear of criticism, leaders too often avoid seeking feedback. Let's not allow ourselves to shy away from the gift of being able to see ourselves as others see us.

Leaders often make one or more of the following mistakes when receiving feedback:

- Receive feedback as a personal attack and respond defensively or simply discard the feedback in its entirety
- Take feedback personally and then severely doubt themselves because they're too hard on themselves after hearing the feedback
- Tell themselves that the feedback is biased and, therefore, discard it

As you can imagine, these responses are counter-productive to mastering the Inner Game of Leadership. Keep in mind that it is such a gift to be able to see yourself as others see you. If we choose to cherish that gift and extract the learning from it, we will be able to greatly accelerate our learning as a leader as we strive to master our Inner Game of Leadership.

Best-selling author Don Miguel Ruiz wrote a wonderful book called, *The Four Agreements*. The book captures Toltec wisdom passed down over many generations. One of the four agreements the book highlights is, "Don't take anything personally." When we take things personally, we step onto the roller coaster of our never-ending cycle of reactivity. Some might say we need to develop a thicker skin. I don't like that saying as it implies stoicism rather than mindfulness. What I like to say is to never take anything personally, mindfully look for any and all truth in the feedback, and then use that truth to fuel ourselves to take our leadership to the next level.

Much is to be gained by facing up to truths about ourselves, but we need to calibrate our minds to more accurately see ourselves before we can openly and non-defensively see our flaws and our strengths. Those of us who beat ourselves up the most are the ones most likely to get defensive and not truly hear any difficult feedback. Sometimes our own internal dialog is so cruel and distorted that we end up being too fragile in the face of any criticism from others. Cultivating robust and supportive internal self-talk is critical for our unshakeable influence in many ways. Nowhere is it more important than being able to hear critical feedback from others without either crumbling inside or roaring back with righteous defensiveness.

When it comes to gathering feedback from others, I recommend a relatively continuous stream of real-time feedback from key stakeholders in your success. This includes, of course, your boss. It also includes at least a portion of your direct reports if not all of them. It's also most helpful to include some of your peers in your feedback loop.

In terms of frequency, I recommend a best practice of having feedback conversations at least once per month. This may sound like a lot, but it's really important to hold this as a regular dialog. The longer the time after feedback, the less useful and actionable it is to us. As a rule of thumb, the more continuous the feedback, the better.

In my experience, leaders more quickly maximize their influence by taking advantage of some of the best leadership feedback tools available. Thus, I also recommend a best practice of using formal, 360-degree feedback mechanisms on a yearly cadence. One of the tools we use most often with our clients is the Leadership Circle Profile 360. Not only is it a great 360, it also aligns very well with mastering the Inner Game of Leadership that this book advocates.

It's important for us to learn to embrace all feedback as a gift and look for the truth in what's being said even if it was delivered poorly. Our meditation practice will help us to receive feedback constructively and not take it personally. We can shift our self-talk anytime we find ourselves taking feedback personally, and we can use our inner Heartset skills to constructively navigate any emotional reaction we may have to hearing feedback.

Questions for reflection:

- How can I be grateful for all feedback?
- How can I be more self-compassionate when receiving feedback so that I don't take it personally?
- Am I taking on a victim Mindset when receiving feedback? If so, how can I shift my Mindset to that of a co-creator?
- How can I use my conscious, heart-based listening skills to take in feedback?

GIVE FEEDBACK AS OFTEN AS POSSIBLE

Just like receiving feedback from others is one of the best gifts you can give yourself, giving regular feedback to others is also one of the best gifts you can give to those who work for, with, or around you. If you can build the skill of giving feedback in a way that most people experience as positive, constructive, and inspiring, you will be far ahead of the leadership competition because so many executives really struggle with giving feedback well.

We all need transparent and regular feedback to thrive. Just like receiving feedback is a gift, giving feedback is also a gift. The challenge is that many people are sensitive to feedback and struggle to receive it constructively. If we can give feedback in a way that champions other people with discernment instead of judgment and balances positive traits with areas for improvement, we will tend to cultivate in others the ability to be appreciative of the opportunity for growth and learning that feedback offers them.

There are two primary aspects to delivering feedback well. One has to do with our choice of words when delivering feedback. This is a topic that has been well covered by other books. (Please see the resources section of this book for information on that.) The second important aspect in delivering feedback well is our way of being – who we are being on the inside – when we communicate it.

Recall that 60-80% of the impact we have on others is non-verbal. In my experience, when people are stressed (as they often are when receiving feedback), our non-verbal communication becomes even more important. In other words, our inner state when delivering feedback typically matters more than how we word the feedback we give. We need to have significant mastery over our Inner Game of Leadership to do this well. If we're feeling anxious, angry, or in any way distracted while giving feedback, the receiver's stress will likely be amplified. We need to be in a place of inner calm and compassion, so we can champion them as much as possible.

Recall also that people have a negativity bias and will more likely flourish when their experience of us is such that they have a positive:negative experience ratio of about 5:1. That doesn't mean that any specific feedback conversation necessarily needs to follow that ratio. In fact, it might come across as forced and artificial if we attempted to say five positive things before the one negative thing. If we realize as we're about to share some difficult feedback that our positive:negative ratio is off, it's too late to do anything about it. That's why we need to be proactively creating positive experiences for others. In doing so, one of the things we're accomplishing is building a relationship that includes difficult feedback that the other person is more likely to receive well and take constructive action on.

When giving feedback it is especially important for us to optimize our internal state. We must use our inner Heartset skills to be in a calm and non-attached place. We also want to use our relational Heartset skills to monitor others' emotions and support them in navigating their own emotional reactions to the feedback they're hearing. At the same time, recognize that you are likely still learning how to give feedback constructively. As such, you will make mistakes. Treat yourself with self-compassion when you do screw up, and do your best to make amends with others as needed.

Questions for reflection:

- How is this feedback you're about to give helpful and constructive for the other person?
- Have you proactively invested in the positive:negative ratio such that this person can more easily hear the feedback in a constructive way?
- What do you need to do to be in a calm and grounded inner state when giving feedback?
- How will you navigate your own emotions and the emotions of others as you give this feedback?
- How can you practice discernment without judgment as you provide this feedback?
- Is your Mindset that of a persecutor/villain? How can you shift it to a challenger/champion?
- Is your Mindset that of a rescuer/hero? How can you shift it to a coach/mentor?

PRACTICE GOOD MEETING HYGIENE

So much time is wasted in organizations because of the tolerated cultural norms around meetings. When working with clients, I will often do a deep dive into meeting hygiene because there's so much opportunity for improved productivity, efficiency, and decision-making.

From a tactical perspective, the issues highlighted in this section are straightforward to fix. From the standpoint of changing cultural norms, it becomes harder. The difficulty lies not so much in knowing how to do it better. Most savvy leaders are clear enough about how to do it. The difficulty typically arises because not enough people are willing to take a stand for better meeting hygiene. From the perspective of mastering our Inner Game of Leadership to maximize our influence, we must start with ourselves and lead by example.

So, I am providing you with some checklists to get you thinking about your own choices regarding the meeting culture of your organization, and how you can improve that meeting culture by shifting your own habits first.

To help you self-identify your organization's meeting culture, here's a check-list of questions designed to illuminate some of your company's meeting hygiene issues:

- Do you ever call meetings without a clear agenda disseminated in advance?
- Do you allow meetings to go too far off track?
- Do you influence meetings to be solution-focused rather than problem-focused?
- Do your meetings ever end without clear outcomes and tangible action items to move the agenda forward?
- Do you hold people accountable to what they agreed to accomplish in between meetings?
- Do you default to 60-minute meetings, or do you mindfully choose meeting length given the topic?
- Do you ask yourself whether or not a meeting is truly necessary? For example, perhaps a series of 1:1 conversations is a better use of everyone's time?
- Do you default to inviting too many people to a meeting just to make sure nobody misses anything?
- Do you attend meetings that you don't really and truly need to be in?
- Do you send subordinates to meetings whenever possible (assuming your team's attendance is truly required)?
- Do you make sure you carve out time in your calendar for strategic thinking and getting stuff done, or do you allow your calendar to fill up with back-to-back meetings?
- Do you start and end meetings on time?

- Are you fully present in meetings, or are you checking email, looking at your phone, working on something else or daydreaming?
- Are the other meeting participants fully present for meetings, or are they checking email on their phone, working on something else, etc.?

I expect we can all relate to many of these issues. Perhaps even all of them. The payoff here is potentially large. Please review again the list above and imagine how much more satisfied, productive, and effective you and your team would be if you took all these steps. Now, imagine if your entire organization was vigilant in these ways.

We must first do our part by leading by example and setting our own teams up for maximum success with a healthy meeting culture. Once we have our own house in order, we can begin to influence other teams to improve their meeting culture as well.

Questions for reflection:

- How willing are you to say no?
- How willing are you to take a stand for better meeting hygiene in service to driving up everyone's productivity and effectiveness?
- Are you taking a victim Mindset in regard to your organization's meeting culture? How can you shift to a co-creator Mindset instead?
- How can you practice discernment without judgment as you advocate for better meeting hygiene in your organization?

How to Increase Your Influence with Senior Executives

In my experience as an executive coach and keynote speaker, I know this question is on the minds of many leaders. Here are some tips to help you apply the learning of this book to this important topic.

1) How you carry yourself is what matters the most.

No one else will believe in you until you believe in yourself. Put another way, why would anyone trust someone that doesn't trust themselves? Influencing senior executives is one of the places where mastering your Inner Game of Leadership pays off in spades. Use your improved Mindset and Heartset to develop more conviction in the value of your own point of view while also clearly honoring others' voices.

2) Meet them where they're at.

Anytime you're communicating, you need to make every effort to understand their point of view and frame what you say in terms that honor their priorities. It's up to you to take the lead when it comes to both proactively asking yourself what an executive's biggest priorities are before speaking with them and also improving your skills of reading people in the moment and improvising or adjusting what you say and how you say it based on what you're sensing from them.

Also, as you're working to better meet senior executives where they're at, keep in mind that senior executives:

- Likely have a more strategic and high-level view than you
- Are **extremely** busy
- Need you to be succinct, to the point, and solution-focused
- Have a million priorities, and you're just one of them

If you're unable to influence an executive in the direction that you think best serves your organization, *that is your fault.* You need to adjust what you're doing to better meet them where they're at, so they're more likely to hear and understand what you're trying to communicate. Of course, communication is always co-created, but it's most helpful to focus on what you can control—yourself.

3) Proactively aim to provide insight in every conversation.

In today's racetrack-paced world, everyone is super-busy, and no one is busier than a senior executive. Executives are constantly being pulled in a million directions, and it seems like everyone wants a piece of their time. When you have a chance to interact with a senior executive, you may only get a few minutes. Make those minutes count. Prepare in advance some unique and concise insights you want to share with specific executives and be ready to share them when the opportunity arises. If you don't proactively offer valuable insights to senior executives on a consistent basis, you will likely disappear into the white noise of the many people they interact with on a daily basis.

4) Be willing to speak the difficult truth.

When I tell people this, the first reaction I most often see is fear. I can immediately sense their worry about the potential consequences of sharing a difficult truth with a senior executive. Remember that one of the biggest challenges senior executives face is gaining access to timely and accurate information about what is really going on in the organization. By the time information gets to them, it has almost invariably been watered down, filtered, and delayed so many times that it's almost completely useless. If you've ever wondered why senior executive decisions can sometimes seem out of alignment with what is truly going on in the business, this is one of the key reasons. In essence, every organization will be higher functioning when the truth is valued more than looking good.

But let's get back to that fear you might be feeling around this. The first thing to know is that your fear is very likely blown out of proportion. Take a look at your self-talk. Is it distorted? How can you shift yourself to a more positive and empowered Mindset and Heartset? Second, if you practice discernment without judgment and communicate without blame and then explain your position in a concise and thoughtful manner, most executives will be thankful for your directness and insight. Third, consider that you're actually not doing your job properly if you consciously withhold what you deem to be critical information for the organization to thrive at its best. Last, on the off chance that your worst fears do come true and there's some sort of retribution, that is a clear signal that this environment may not be the best place for you. If that sounds harsh, ask yourself why would you ever want to spend your precious life working in a place that doesn't suit you?

5) Persistence and calm confidence.

Influence is a marathon, not a sprint. You, your organization, and your senior executive team will be best served by you using your improved Mindset and Heartset skills to remain calm, non-reactive, and constructive in the face of any adversity. Whatever levels of frustration, worry, disappointment, etc. you might feel at times in your journey to be more influential, use your improved emotional intelligence to process and productively express those feelings yourself rather than unconsciously acting them out. And deepen your practice of self-soothing so you become better equipped to return to a non-reactive and grounded state as quickly as possible.

Questions for reflection:

- Are you putting senior executives on a pedestal? If so, how can you learn to think of them as just another flawed human being?
- Are you approaching senior executives from the Drama Paradigm or from the Empowerment Paradigm? How can you approach executives from the Empowerment Paradigm?
- Is your self-talk as you approach an executive supportive of you being your best self? If not, how can you shift your self-talk to support you in making the best impression on senior executives?

INNER GAME OF BEING ON STAGE: BEING AT YOUR BEST WHEN IT REALLY COUNTS

No more powerful an opportunity to influence, inspire, and motivate others exists than to be on stage. The stakes are rarely higher.

If that presentation goes great, it can mean:

- Getting everyone aligned behind your vision and thrilled to be a part of it
- Selling millions of dollars' worth of your services or products
- Getting your new business venture funded
- Securing that next big promotion
- Ensuring (or not) the very success of your company at a crucial inflection point
- Anything and everything related to making your dent in the universe

As you can imagine, it is your Inner Game of Leadership that is key to being at your best when it really counts.

If you're relaxed, willing to be vulnerable, and have confidence in what you're saying and who you are, that will shine through to your audience. If you're anxious, worried, overconfident, or holding back in any way, that will shine through to your audience.

Put simply, performing on stage in front of an audience will completely expose the current health of your Inner Game of Leadership. Every. Single. Time.

Here are five techniques that I've seen work well:

1. Practice, practice, practice.

You have to practice a lot to master anything. If you're fearful of public speaking, then practice becomes even more important. Just any old practice isn't enough; you want to be as mindful as possible in how you go about practicing.

Here are a few tips on how to practice deliberately: Work on just one or two specific things each time you're on stage. If you try to work on more than that, you will likely overwhelm yourself. Make sure you start with the highest leverage points in your growth. Look for the weakest point in your Inner Game of Leadership; that is one place where you likely have the most to gain. Consider enrolling in a public speaking program, acting or improvisation course. Recall the power of giving yourself the gift of feedback by having yourself filmed as you are on stage.

2. Change your self-talk to be more positive.

Keep in mind that the more vulnerable an activity feels to us, the more distorted and cruel our self-talk tends to be. For most people, there is nothing that feels more vulnerable than being on stage. Use the best friend self-talk exercise from Chapter 5 to shift your inner dialog to be more positive and constructive.

3. Get into your body and out of your head.

If you're worrying about how you look or how you sound, then you will tend to come across as tentative, uncertain, and anxious. Your audience will automatically tend to feel your feelings. Is that the way you want them to feel? But it's one thing to know that you need to think positive, and it's another to quickly shift yourself to a more positive place.

It's often helpful to do something that will get you into your body right before you get on stage. What I've seen work well for people are things like jumping up and down, swinging your arms around, making silly sounds, or anything else that will get your blood flowing. That may sound embarrassing to you. If you can find a "safe" place to do it, then do it that way. If not, do it anyway or maybe do something that might feel safer like stretching, arching your back, smiling broadly, opening your arms widely, etc.

Most great speakers also create a physical warm-up routine and then they do that routine every time before going on stage. The repetition, comfort, and association of those physical movements go a long way toward putting us in a positive inner state in a relatively automatic way.

4. Practice gratitude.

Every time you are on stage, take a few minutes afterwards to write down at least three specific things you did well. Recall that our brains are wired to over-emphasize negative experiences and under-emphasize positive ones. By taking the time to highlight what went well, you will cultivate more appreciation of the stage skills you already have. That more positive Mindset will help you to enjoy the experience more and better equip you to learn each time you're on stage. It's important that you actually write this down and not just run through it in your mind. It will feel more real to you when you write about it, and you will retain that positive memory more solidly. It may be helpful to review the gratitude section in Chapter 4 as you practice gratitude for being on stage.

5. View each and every time you're on stage as a learning experience.

Life is a constant learning experience. We're meant to learn and grow our entire lives. If we ever fully "arrived" and stopped striving for more learning and more growth, we'd be incredibly bored. Embrace lifelong learning by looking at everything in your life - no matter how uncomfortable or painful it may sometimes be - as a learning experience. And have fun! The more you're enjoying your experience, the more you will allow yourself to learn, and the better you will come across to your audience.

Questions for reflection:

- What kind of warm-up routine do you want to create for yourself before each presentation?
- What is one specific skill you want to work on the next time you present? How will you practice that?
- How can you use your Heartset skills to maximize your emotional impact when speaking?

What Do You Do After You Blow It?

In today's world where we are nearly always moving at racetrack speeds, mistakes will happen. And when they do, things can go bad very quickly. We simply can't afford **not** to build our recovery muscles. Like anything else in leadership, recovering from failure is a skill that can be developed when you focus on it.

Here's a five-step process to practice when things don't go as planned:

1. Stay present.

Hey, you just screwed up. Stay with it. Don't try to pretend it didn't happen. You can only learn from your mistakes when you let yourself fully experience them. Take a few deep breaths and recognize that screwing up is an integral part of your learning curve. Practice self-compassion. What would you say to your best friend if they just made a mistake?

2. Celebrate your failure.

Recall that failure is a Mindset, not an outcome. Borrowing from improvisational theater, celebrate failure. I imagine that might sound a bit odd. Welcoming and celebrating failure is a great way to counteract our years of conditioning to stigmatize it. The only way to get more comfortable taking risks is to get more comfortable with the possibility of failure. One easy and effective way to celebrate failure is to smile when you believe you've failed.

3. Acknowledge it openly.

When you screw up publicly, you actually have a great opportunity to have a positive impact on those around you. If you acknowledge it openly and with no shame or stigma, it's as if the whole room breathes a subconscious sigh of relief. No one likes worrying about looking bad. If you don't appear to be worried about it, others are more likely to think maybe it's not so bad to make a mistake after all.

Acknowledging your failure openly can be a bit cathartic for everyone, including you.

4. Learn from it.

While you may not have time in the moment, do take a little time to replay the mistake, only with an eye to learn from it. This can be tricky, as replaying the mistake in our minds can lead to cruel and distorted self-talk, and that will lead us to feel more ashamed of it.

One way to counteract the tendency to beat yourself up is to think about all the things you did right. With nearly any mistake there are plenty of things that you did right. Use gratitude to list those things. Then, look at the mistake holistically. See what you could improve at while also owning what you did right.

5. Move back into action.

While you certainly want to think about what you can do better next time, don't get stuck in reflecting on it or beating yourself up. Learn the key lessons from your mistake and get back into action sooner rather than later. You simply can't afford to stay stuck. The racetrack is still there, and all the other leaders and organizations are passing you by while you stay stuck.

Questions for reflection:

- Where does your self-talk go when you make a mistake? Does it support you or tear you down? How can you be more self-compassionate when you make a mistake?
- How can you be grateful for failure?
- How will you celebrate failure to yourself?
- What do you want to model for others when it comes to owning your mistakes, learning from them, and mindfully moving back into action?

Chapter 13

Winning the Leadership Race with Your Practice

WHEN I WAS RACING motorcycles, one of the key reasons why I was so good at it right off the bat was I immediately put a ***ton*** of time into practicing all the different aspects of what it takes to be competitive in motorcycle road-racing. So, in a way, I was not great at it right away. It just appeared that way to the casual observer because I immediately put a lot of time, effort, and money into making myself and my motorcycle the best they could possibly be.

And I didn't just throw money and time at the problem. I very consciously made choices to differentiate myself and my motorcycle from my competition. For example, in motorcycle road-racing, one of the key components to going as fast as possible is the suspension of the motorcycle. Fast engines matter, of course, but all the horsepower in the world isn't all that helpful if the motorcycle can't maintain traction through the corners.

When I was racing, a number of reputable suspension tuners were available for hire. Nearly all of my competitors did exactly that – hired a reputable suspension tuner. I quickly recognized that if everyone is essentially riding the same suspension setup, then no one will have any suspension advantages. Thus, I took a different tactic and did my own suspension tuning. Suspension tuning has a steep learning curve, and

I spent a lot of time and energy learning how it worked. I also spent a lot of time on the racetrack testing out many different ways of setting up my suspension. There were many practice days on the racetrack where all I did was tune and test my suspension.

In dedicating my time and energy to learning the craft of suspension tuning, I was able to find a competitive advantage, and I believe I had a better-handling motorcycle than most any other motorcycle in my racing division. That enabled me to go through corners with greater speed, more confidence, and less risk of crashing. It became a key competitive edge between me and my competition because I was willing to do what others wouldn't do.

The world has never been more competitive. Technology and globalization have made us more connected than ever before. As a result, competition for the top leadership roles is fiercer than it's ever been. The leaders who win the leadership race of the 21st century will be those who put in the time, mindfully practicing their leadership game day-in and day-out. Those who don't will be disrupted. It's just a matter of when.

Returning to our model of reactivity, as you put these skills to use more and more, you will find yourself becoming higher and higher functioning. With enough practice, you will get to a place where you end up spending nearly all of your time at your highest level of functioning. You will always have some level of fluctuation in your performance level and mood, but those swings will become smaller and your level of functioning will be concentrated mostly at the upper end of your range.

Figure 13.1 illustrates what will be happening for you next with consistent and mindful practice that maximizes your Inner Game of Leadership. The dark line shows that you're now operating mostly at the level of an emotional high. Further, from this new experience will come new awareness. You can now see that there's a higher truth you can live by that allows you to function at a higher level nearly all the time. From this vantage point, you can now also clearly see that the reality of circumstances is a lower truth, and that your old, emotional lows were based on a false truth.

Higher Truth
Emotional High

Lower Truth
Reality of
circumstances

False Truth
Emotional Low

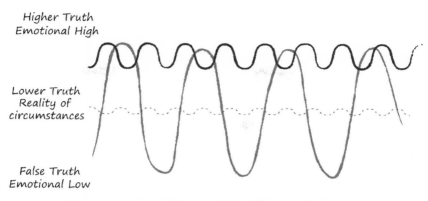

Figure 13.1 – Reactivity Model with Enough Practice

Conclusion

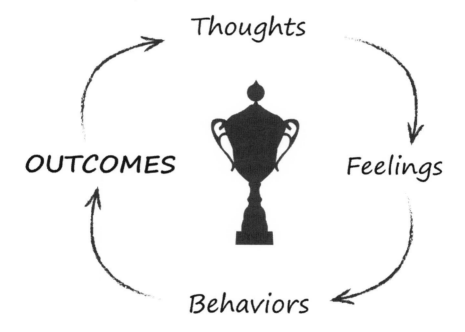

LEADERSHIP IN A **VUCA** WORLD

THE MORE YOU MASTER your Inner Game of Leadership by improving and optimizing your thoughts, feelings, and behaviors, the more your outcomes will improve, too. At the same time, the next – and ultimately the most important – step of outcomes is completely up to you.

If you do nothing with what you've read in this book, the only thing that will happen in your life is that you will eventually give away or discard this book and, thus, create room for the next book you read (and eventually discard that book after doing nothing with it either).

You simply didn't pick up this book and go on this adventure with me because you were satisfied with the status quo of your Inner Game of Leadership. You picked up this book because you were dissatisfied with your Inner Game of Leadership and you want to attain deeper mastery over it so you can be a better leader in our VUCA world.

For inspiration to make this change in your leadership and life, I strongly encourage you to do an internet search for "Dead Poets Society carpe diem scene" and watch the approximately three-minute clip now. I know of no more inspiring scene to fuel you to make the most of your life.

Your time is now. If not now, then when?

WINNING, TROPHIES, AND LEADERSHIP – WHAT DOES IT ALL MEAN?

More than 15 years have passed since I last raced a motorcycle. Recently, I decided to let go of some of my "less meaningful" motorcycle racing trophies. I put less meaningful in quotes because each trophy represents many hours of practice working both on my craft as a racer and on the motorcycle itself. Constant tinkering and striving for improvement. Constant thinking about how to go just that little bit faster. And then that little bit faster again, and that little bit faster again, and again until I began to find myself winning races and trophies. Constant striving, striving, striving, until eventually I was able to come home with a trophy representing excellence. A whole lot of blood, sweat, and tears were poured into each and every one of my trophies. Letting any one of them go wasn't easy. But I have come to a place of seeing my trophies and the experience of racing and winning very differently.

But first, let's go back to the beginning. I started racing motorcycles mostly because I thought it would be fun. It seemed to me like it would be cool to be able to ride as fast as possible on a racetrack under controlled conditions where I could really explore the limits of what was possible for me and my motorcycle. I didn't start off thinking all that much about winning. What I was thinking about was having fun and exploring the limits of what I could do.

And then I did much better in my first race than I imagined I would. And then even better in my next race. I was probably only a couple races into my racing career when I saw just how possible it seemed that I could be good at this – perhaps even great at it. After that, placing well and striving to win became a primary focus.

At that point in my life, I had already participated in many different sports. I was always drawn to adrenaline-filled and individual sports like downhill snow-skiing, snowboarding, mountain-biking, skydiving, bungee jumping, and SCUBA diving. I've also been an avid hiker and played doubles volleyball (my only real endeavor into team sports), even managing to win a couple of volleyball tournaments in spite of my very average stature. I was, in no uncertain terms, athletically inclined and had spent many hours in activities that taught me how to be comfortable in my body, how to be fully present, and how to focus on the task at hand.

Yet I had experienced only a few fleeting moments of feeling like I was truly great at any of it. And in the heat of competition, I sometimes didn't do well due to my mental game. I always felt like a bit of an outsider and struggled to believe I could be great at anything. On the outside it probably appeared I had it all together and was very calm and cool doing all these sports. On the inside, my experience was a different story.

It's fascinating to look back on the person I was when I first embarked on my motorcycle racing adventure. I was so hungry for more from myself, but I didn't know how to get there. I honestly felt like I was my own worst enemy in many ways. Too often harshly critical of myself. Too often neglectful of my own needs. Too often giving up on myself when it got hard. While I was in my thirties at the time I started racing motorcycles, I still needed to prove to myself and to the world that I could be great at something. And that thing was about to become motorcycle road-racing. I didn't realize when I started racing motorcycles just how important that journey of motorcycle road-racing would become for me.

You've already heard a number of the highs and lows of my motorcycle-racing career. In the end, I didn't walk away with that season championship. But I did walk away with a number of race wins, was a true contender for that championship, and achieved a large number of podium finishes. **Most importantly, I walked away with my pride fully restored.** I had finally come to believe that I was, and always could be, great. At that point in my life, my ego needed that series of motorcycle race wins and great success in a highly touted sport to fully feel like a whole person.

Much of this book has been about how leadership, life, and business are **not** all about winning, and how too much focus on winning can be problematic to functioning at our best. All of this is true.

And what is also true is that winning can be wonderful. Winning can be a way to fulfill our ego's needs. Ego can drive us to excel in ways that we couldn't otherwise. Up to a point, ego is good, but at some point, it becomes a limiting factor. Recall that in my first race win, it was when I thought (and wholeheartedly believed) on that very last lap of the race that I'm already a winner no matter how I finish, that I went faster than ever before and achieved a track lap time record that still stands to this day.

It's when ego over-drives us and/or others around us that it can very much get in the way of performing at our best. There is another story from the final season of my motorcycle racing days that illustrates this point.

You see, that fateful day when I crashed at 100 mph was not the final nail in the coffin for me to be able to win the championship that year. The final nail in the coffin happened in the very next race.

The race after my big crash came about a month later. By then, I'd had plenty of time to reflect on my situation and become clear about what it would take to win the championship given my new situation: for the first time, I was substantially behind in the points for the season.

I was under a lot of pressure. To be able to win the championship I needed to win every remaining race, and even that would not be enough to ensure my victory. I also needed my biggest rival to have at least one bad day where he was off the podium – not a typical finish for him at all.

Leading up to the race, I felt the pressure. I felt the pressure of not knowing if I could do it. I felt the pressure of how having another bad day, or even just a less-than-great day, would most likely completely ruin any hope of winning that championship. I simply **had** to do really well that day – **or else**.

The racetrack we were racing at that day is called Sonoma Raceway; it is one of the most difficult and dangerous tracks in the United States. It's also a track where I had always excelled. I had won the first two races here that season by wide margins. I was used to winning at this racetrack, and there wasn't any reason why I shouldn't win again.

But when the green flag dropped signaling the start of the race, I was clearly not at my best. I got off the line sluggishly and was in something like 5th spot on the first lap, in spite of being gridded in 2nd place at the start. Normally that wouldn't be too much of a problem at this track, as I was often able to pass people here without too much delay. But the pressure I was putting on myself was limiting my performance.

As I try to recall more specifics of that race now, I realize that the specifics are very foggy in my memory. I remember other races where I won or placed well very vividly, even all these years later. The fogginess of my memory of this particular race is a clear signal of how blocked and under-performing I was.

What I do remember for much of that race is feeling tentative and struggling to do my best. Again, the self-inflicted pressure was killing my performance compared to what I was capable of. In short, I was playing not to lose instead of playing to win. Fast forward a number of painful laps to the final lap of the race and something began to change inside of me. The urgency of the situation became more apparent. I was still in 5th place, and if I finished the race in that position, any realistic chance of winning the championship would be gone. At this late stage of a race, the leaders are typically contending with lapping the slowest racers. With a lot of lap traffic, racers often have to slow down to safely pass slower racers.

To this day I am not sure why or how I was able to shift my Mindset, but in turn number 6 at Sonoma Raceway (a.k.a. "the carousel") I saw an opportunity and capitalized on it. This turn is a long, fast, downward-sloping, bumpy and slightly off-camber 180-degree corner that comes just before the longest straightaway on this racetrack. As far as lap times go, this is one of the most crucial corners to get right on this track, and it had always been one of my favorites. Remember how much time and energy I put into tuning the suspension on my motorcycle? This corner, as one of the trickiest corners we ever raced, was my test corner for all that suspension tuning. It was when I got my suspension working extremely well on this corner that it began working well nearly everywhere.

On that last lap heading into the carousel, I was in 5th place with the race leader off in the distance ahead of me. It was seemingly impossible at this point to catch up with only about half a lap remaining. Going through the carousel, the four racers ahead of me got held up by lapped traffic. I saw an opportunity to weave my way through traffic without losing any speed. I hit a small opening in the lapped traffic and got on the gas extra early so that I could maximize my speed onto the long straight. I was able to pass into 4th place in the carousel itself (passing my biggest rival for the championship in the process), and then, as I transitioned off the carousel and onto the long straightaway, I knew I was carrying more speed than I've ever carried out of that corner.

But first place was still so far away that it seemed impossible to catch up. And then, to my surprise, I was able to pass into 3rd place, and then into 2nd place. But 1st place was still a long way ahead of me. Somehow, I was able to pass into the lead while braking into turn 7. It was a miraculous save from what would have been a disastrous day – or so I thought.

As I made my way through the rest of that lap, I was able to pull out a bit of a lead, probably about .5 seconds of a lead heading into the final corner of the race. Typically, with just one corner remaining and that big of a lead, the race would be won easily. But the opponent I'd passed just a few corners earlier had a different idea. He had led most of the race for the first time in his road-racing career. I can understand how it would be disappointing to be passed convincingly on the final lap and how a racer doesn't want to give up the lead, especially so late in the race.

The final corner of that racetrack was the slowest corner on the track. The speed through it was less than 50 mph. We were coming into that corner from one of the fastest parts of the track where we'd just been going around 100 mph. Needless to say, it's hard-braking entry into that corner. This racer attempted to pass me on the brakes while carrying so much entry speed that he couldn't possibly make the apex of the corner. It happened in such a way that I had a choice of either being hit by his bike or running wide – really wide and off the track. I opted to avoid the collision and run wide, knowing that a collision here would very likely take me out of the race entirely.

Eventually, once we were well off the track (but still on the pavement) we still collided. Somehow, in spite of being tossed up in the air off of my bike, I managed not to crash. But he did crash. Fortunately, I was able to avoid the carnage of his crash and get back on the racetrack and finish the race.

But so much time had passed while all this was happening that I ended up finishing 4th in a race that I should have won. And my biggest rival for the season championship won the race – the only race he ever won at Sonoma. After what I thought was a miraculous save was a disastrous finish. My chances of winning the championship were now completely gone. The racer who nearly took me out was given a warning by the officials over dangerous riding, but the damage that was done during that race could not be undone.

In the months after that race, I had a really hard time processing what happened. It felt so unfair. But with time, I have come to see it differently. Honestly, it is only with the writing of this book more than 15 years later that I have fully processed it. Yes, it was unfair. Yes, it shouldn't have happened that way. But it did happen that way, and life isn't always fair.

Here's the thing: when I looked at everyone's lap times after that race, everyone else had run their usual pace. It was me who was unusually slow for all but the last lap of that race. If I'd been on my game from the very beginning of the race, I would have won by a wide margin, and no one could have possibly taken me out because they wouldn't have been anywhere near me. While the ending of that race felt unfair, it was my own self-limiting performance that day that made the unhappy ending possible.

One thing – plain and simple – led to my under-performance that day: my out-of-control ego beating me up and over-driving me. I was defining my value as a person on how that race went. In doing so, I ironically under-performed and made that disastrous ending possible.

It's a paradox or, at least, a razor's edge. The drive to win can lead us to new heights we could never achieve without competition and the drive to be the "best." And that same drive to win can also cause us to under-perform when we base too much of our self-esteem on winning. Competition is meant to bring out the best in us. And it often does. There is no way I ever would have gone so fast on a motorcycle if it wasn't for competition and wanting to beat my competitors.

My relationship to winning, and my coveted trophies, has shifted since then. On the one hand, some part of me needed that experience of being great at something. Some part of me really needed to prove to myself and to the world that I could do it. On the other hand, once I got there and achieved much of what I set out to do (except that damn championship!), I had a different experience. What I experienced was feeling more confident and going even faster on the racetrack when I stopped over-driving myself and started thinking of myself as a winner no matter what the outcome.

Winning is still meaningful to me. My trophies are still meaningful to me. But now my trophies don't just represent winning at any cost. They represent the pursuit of excellence. They represent believing in myself no matter what. They represent relationships with others because competition doesn't exist without others, and I never could have excelled as much as I did without strong relationships all around me – including with my fellow competitors. The trophies also represent what is possible for me – and for anyone – when we put our mind, heart, soul and everything we've got into being the very best we can be. The sky is the limit when we really and fully commit to something. To me, competition no longer means winning all the time. I'm already a winner no matter what. And ironically, from that place of not hanging my very self-worth on it, I'm so much more capable of winning.

To let go of some of my motorcycle racing trophies, I had to see the whole experience in a new light. I now see that period of my life as an all-important set of milestones that made the next part of my life possible. Since retiring from racing, I have been more committed to living a life of purpose, meaning and making the biggest contribution I can make in this lifetime – because my life became about so much more than just winning trophies. At the same time, I needed that experience in order for the next parts of my life to become possible.

Carl Jung said, "The first half of life is devoted to forming a healthy ego, the second half is going inward and letting go of it." The complete forming of a healthy ego only came for me when I won those motorcycle races. I'm not sure there was any other way for me to get there. And I'm not sure anyone who's being honest with themselves doesn't also need their own personal version of winning motorcycle races to completely form their healthy ego before they can move into the next stage of their leadership and life journey.

WHAT'S NEXT IN MASTERING YOUR INNER GAME OF LEADERSHIP

Ironically, part of what it takes to become unshakeable in your influence is to recognize that you will never become 100% unshakeable. What is outlined in this book are lifelong practices that you will never completely perfect. But if you commit yourself to the practices of mastering your Inner Game of Leadership, you will eventually get to a place where you are consistently operating at or near the highest end of your capacity all the time.

This is when you will have really let go of the roller coaster of your never-ending cycle of reactivity and set yourself free for your next level of development. You see, about 70-80% of all adults operate primarily in this cycle of reactivity. Once you learn to transcend your reactivity, a whole new way of living and leading opens up to you. This is the place where you feel very comfortable navigating VUCA. You also deal with conflict adeptly – in fact, conflict is just a natural part of your day, and you enter into true servant leadership that serves your organization, yourself, and the community at large.

To help you understand this, figure C.1 shows how you've now reached escape velocity from your reactivity. When you reach that escape velocity, the model of reactivity no longer runs you.

From here, your higher truth line is your new foundation. You now rarely, if ever, fall below your higher truth. And when you do, you recover quickly to functioning from the higher truth. Back to functioning from your biggest capacity. While you still recognize the model of reactivity because it drove your behavior for so long, you no longer live in this model.

The new model you now live in looks nothing like the model of reactivity. It is open, expansive, and filled with connection, possibility, and humble confidence. From here, resilience and servant leadership are now your normal operating modes. You automatically see things in terms of what's best for everyone rather than what's best for you or your immediate team, or even your entire company. You see things more holistically. You rarely get caught up in any drama or reactivity. Instead, you have a calming effect that consistently invites people out of their reactivity and drama and into their higher selves. This territory is where your presence as a leader catalyzes change, inspires people to do their best work, and often leads to the very best outcomes for everyone. You no longer think in terms of a zero-sum game. You now automatically assume there's always a win-win-win for all. Your ego no longer needs to prove itself. It's present because you never fully lose it, but it doesn't control you.

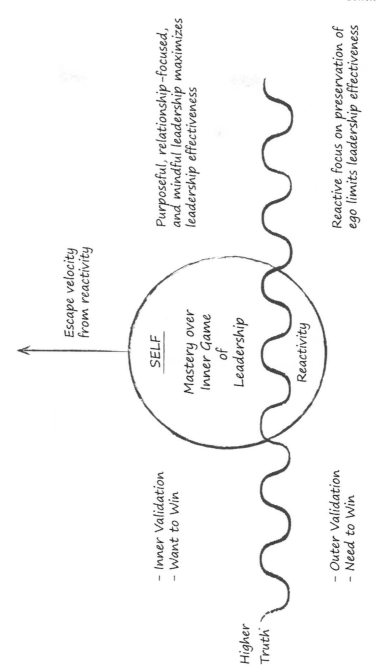

Escape velocity
from reactivity

SELF

Mastery over
Inner Game
of
Leadership

Reactivity

Purposeful, relationship-focused,
and mindful leadership maximizes
leadership effectiveness

Reactive focus on preservation of
ego limits leadership effectiveness

– Inner Validation
– Want to Win

– Outer Validation
– Need to Win

Higher
Truth

Figure C.1 – The Next Levels of Leadership

Every stage of your development creates a whole new level of achievement, inner calm and inspiration within you. This next stage of your development also has you consistently bringing that out in people around you. You may struggle to even imagine this yet because your experience to date has been so different from this. That was your ego and your reactivity driving you. Only when you've sufficiently transcended your reactivity can you move to the next stage of your leadership development.

The New Leadership Paradigm

For decades, centuries perhaps, leadership has been presented as largely *positional*.

Throughout this book, I have challenged the status quo around leadership, arguing that it's critical to adopt a new model of how we think, how we feel, how we behave, and thereby fundamentally shift what it means to be a leader.

My argument is grounded in the idea that to succeed in today's VUCA world, we must switch from seeing leadership as positional to embracing it as relational. We are social creatures, wired to be at our best when we are connected to each other, to ourselves, and to something bigger than us. It is only through leading by relationship that we can consistently enroll, drive, and inspire others to be their very best - *under any and all circumstances*.

The disruption of positional authority by relational authority is already afoot. Not only are you missing a huge opportunity by not treating leadership and relationship as largely synonymous, but if you are not at the forefront of this disruption, you will eventually experience your own form of "ground, sky, ground, sky" – crashing and burning at 100+ mph. Only, it won't be just you tumbling across the racetrack; it may be your entire team or even your entire company. And you may not land without any injuries as I did. You may take out a whole bunch of people with you.

In the race to be the best leader, a new relationship-focused and influence based leadership paradigm is taking hold. The racers are lining up at the starting line. Are you ready to lead in today's VUCA world?

THE END

Reference Notes

(In order of appearance)

CHAPTER 1: THE BUSINESS CASE FOR MASTERING YOUR INNER GAME OF LEADERSHIP

Zwilling, Martin. "On Average, People Work At Less Than 50 Percent Of Their Capacity." Business Insider. Nov. 22, 2010.
https://www.businessinsider.com/on-average-people-work-at-less-than-50-percent-of-their-capacity-2010-11

"North American Employee Turnover: Trends and Effects." Mercer.
https://www.imercer.com/content/article/employee-turnover.aspx

Curtin, Melanie. "In an 8-hour Day, the Average Worker is Productive For This Many Hours." Inc Magazine. July 21, 2016.
https://www.inc.com/melanie-curtin/in-an-8-hour-day-the-average-worker-is-productive-for-this-many-hours.html

Weller, Chris. "Forget the 9 to 5 – Research Suggests There's a Case for the 3 Hour Workday." Business Insider. Sept. 26, 2017
https://www.businessinsider.com/8-hour-workday-may-be-5-hours-too-long-research-suggests-2017-9

Schwantes, Marcel. "Research Discovered This 1 Thing is What Makes Work More Productive and Employees Happier." Inc Magazine. Feb. 16, 2018.
https://www.inc.com/marcel-schwantes/brain-research-discovered-this-1-thing-is-what-makes-work-more-productive-employees-happier.html

Bredberry, Travis. "Why the 8 Hour Workday Doesn't Work." Ladders. Sept 27, 2018.

https://www.theladders.com/career-advice/8-hour-workday-doesnt-work

Carter, Christine. "Why Working Longer Won't Make You More Productive." Greater Good Magazine. Feb. 3, 2016.

https://greatergood.berkeley.edu/article/item/why_working_longer_wont_make_you_more_productive

Fox, Chastity. "Work Institute Releases National Employee Retention Report." The Work Institute. May 1, 2018.

https://workinstitute.com/about-us/news-events/articleid/2259/2018%20retention%20report

"North American Employee Turnover: Trends and Effects." Mercer.

https://www.imercer.com/content/article/employee-turnover.aspx

"Gallup State of the American Manager Report 2018." Gallup.

https://www.gallup.com/services/182138/state-american-manager.aspx

Goler, Lori. Gale, Janelle. Harrington, Brynn. Grant, Adam. "Why People Really Quit Their Jobs." Harvard Business Review. Jan. 11, 2018

https://hbr.org/2018/01/why-people-really-quit-their-jobs

Schwantes, Marcel. "Why Are Your Employees Quitting? A Study Says it Comes Down to Any of These Six Reasons." Inc Magazine. Oct. 23, 2017.

https://www.inc.com/marcel-schwantes/why-are-your-employees-quitting-a-study-says-it-comes-down-to-any-of-these-6-reasons.html

Merhar, Christina. "Employee Retention – The Real Cost of Losing an Employee." Peoplekeep. Feb 4, 2016

https://www.peoplekeep.com/blog/bid/312123/Employee-Retention-The-Real-Cost-of-Losing-an-Employee

Boushey, Heather. Glynn, Sarah Jane. "There are Significant Business Costs to Replacing Employees." Center for American Progress. Nov 16, 2012.

https://www.americanprogress.org/wp-content/uploads/2012/11/
CostofTurnover.pdf

Bersin, Josh. "Employee Retention Now a Big Issue. Why the Tide Has Turned." LinkedIn. Aug 16, 2013.
https://www.linkedin.com/pulse/20130816200159-131079-employee-retention-now-a-big-issue-why-the-tide-has-turned/

O'Boyle, Ernest. Aguinis, Herman. "The Best and the Rest: Revisiting the Norm of Normality of Individual Performance." Personnel Psychology, Wiley Online Library. Feb 27, 2012.
https://onlinelibrary.wiley.com/doi/full/10.1111/j.1744-6570.2011.01239.x

Oakes, Kevin. "How Long Does it Take to Get Fully Productive?" Training Industry Quarterly. Winter 2012.
http://www.nxtbook.com/nxtbooks/trainingindustry/tiq_2012winter/index.php?startid=40#/40

Stibitz, Sara. "How to Get a New Employee up to Speed." Harvard Business Review. May 22, 2015.
https://hbr.org/2015/05/how-to-get-a-new-employee-up-to-speed

"Gallup State of the Global Workplace 2017." Gallup.
https://www.gallup.com/workplace/238079/state-global-workplace-2017.aspx

Murthy, Vivek. "Work and the Loneliness Epidemic." Harvard Business Review. Sept. 26, 2017.
https://hbr.org/cover-story/2017/09/work-and-the-loneliness-epidemic

CHAPTER 2: YOUR SIGHTING LAP FOR THE RACE OF YOUR LIFE

Gladwell, Malcom. *Outliers: The Story of Success.* Little, Brown and Company. Nov 18, 2008.

Peter, Dr. Laurence J. Hull, Raymond. *The Peter Principle: Why Things Always Go Wrong.* William Morrow and Company. 1969.

Goldsmith, Marshall. Reiter, Mark. *What Got You Here, Won't Get You There: How Successful People Become Even More Successful.* Hyperion. Feb. 22, 2007.

Anderson, Robert J. Adams, Williams A. *Mastering Leadership: An Integrated Framework for Breakthrough Performance and Extraordinary Business Results*. Wiley. Nov. 4, 2015.

"Opt Out Policies Increase Organ Donation." Stanford. https://sparq.stanford.edu/solutions/opt-out-policies-increase-organ-donation

"Endowment effect." Wikipedia. https://en.wikipedia.org/wiki/Endowment_effect

"Status Quo Bias." Wikipedia. https://en.wikipedia.org/wiki/Status_quo_bias

"Loss Aversion" https://en.wikipedia.org/wiki/Loss_aversion

Tasler, Nick. "Stop Using the Excuse 'Organizational Change is hard'." Harvard Business Review. July 19, 2017. https://hbr.org/2017/07/stop-using-the-excuse-organizational-change-is-hard%C2%A0

Ewenstein, Boris. Smith, Wesley. Sologar, Ashvin. "Changing Change Management." Mckinsey. July 2015. https://www.mckinsey.com/featured-insights/leadership/changing-change-management

"New Years Resolution Statistics." Statistic Brain Research Institute. https://www.statisticbrain.com/new-years-resolution-statistics/

Day, Douglas. "Reactive Leadership." The Leadership Circle. Nov. 11, 2015. https://leadershipcircle.com/en/reactive-leadership/

CHAPTER 3: INTRODUCTION TO MINDSET

Achor, Shawn. *The Happiness Advantage: How a Positive Brain Fuels Success in Work and Life*. Penguin Random House. Sept. 14, 2010.

Achor, Shawn. The Happy Secret to Better Work. TED. May, 2011. https://www.ted.com/talks/shawn_achor_the_happy_secret_to_better_work

Achor, Shawn. "Positive Intelligence." Harvard Business Review. Jan-Feb 2012 issue.

https://hbr.org/2012/01/positive-intelligence

Dweck, Carol S. "The Power Of Believing That You Can Improve." TED. Nov. 2014.

https://www.ted.com/talks/carol_dweck_the_power_of_believing_that_you_can_improve

Dweck, Carol S. *Mindset: The New Psychology of Success*. Penguin Random House. Dec. 26, 2007.

Lyubomirsky, Sonja. *The How of Happiness: A New Approach to Getting the Life You Want*. Penguin Books. Dec. 30, 2008.

Suval, Lauren. "Happiness and Choices." Psychology Central. Jul. 8, 2018.

https://psychcentral.com/blog/happiness-and-choices/

"Emotional Contagion."

https://en.wikipedia.org/wiki/Emotional_contagion

Raghunathan, Raj. "How Negative is Your Mental Chatter?". Psychology Today. Oct. 10, 2013.

https://www.psychologytoday.com/us/blog/sapient-nature/201310/how-negative-is-your-mental-chatter

University of Southern California Laboratory of Neuroimaging.

https://www.loni.usc.edu

Chopra, Deepak. "The Basics of Quantum Healing: Understanding the True Nature of the Human Body, Mind and Spirit." The Healers Journal. July 13, 2013

http://www.thehealersjournal.com/2013/07/13/the-basics-of-quantum-healing-human-body-mind-and-spirit/

Marano, Hara Estroff. "Depression Doing the Thinking." Psychology Today. June 9, 2016.

https://www.psychologytoday.com/us/articles/200107/depression-doing-the-thinking

Estimate of the possible number of thoughts in a day. Visit this link and click "every-thought"

http://www.aesthetic-machinery.com/every-thing.html

Hawthorne, Jennifer. "Change Your Thoughts, Change Your World."

http://www.jenniferhawthorne.com/articles/change_your_thoughts.html

CHAPTER 4: FOUNDATIONAL MINDSET SKILLS

"Fundamental Attribution Error."
https://en.wikipedia.org/wiki/Fundamental_attribution_error
"Nervous System."
https://en.wikipedia.org/wiki/Nervous_system
"Autonomic Nervous System"
https://en.wikipedia.org/wiki/Autonomic_nervous_system
"Parasympathetic Nervous System Vs Sympathetic Nervous System."
    Diffen.com.
https://www.diffen.com/difference/Parasympathetic_nervous_
    system_vs_Sympathetic_nervous_system
Hanson, Rick. *Hardwiring Happiness: The New Brain Science of Contentment, Calm, and Confidence.* Harmony. Oct. 8, 2013.
Ireland, Tom. "What Does Mindfulness Meditation Do to Your Brain?"
    Scientific American. June 12, 2014.
https://blogs.scientificamerican.com/guest-blog/what-does-mindfulness-meditation-do-to-your-brain/
Schulte, Brigid. "Harvard Neuroscientist: Meditation Not Only Reduces Stress, Here's How it Changes Your Brain." Washington Post. May 26, 2015.
https://www.washingtonpost.com/news/inspired-life/wp/2015/05/26/harvard-neuroscientist-meditation-not-only-reduces-stress-it-literally-changes-your-brain/?utm_term=.223123d2f441
Gaffney, Maureen. "Positive Charge." Irish Times. Nov. 5, 2011.
https://www.irishtimes.com/life-and-style/people/positive-charge-1.8048
Gordon, Amie M. "The Science of Flourishing – It's in the Numbers."
    Psychology Today. June 7, 2013.
https://www.psychologytoday.com/us/blog/between-you-and-me/201306/the-science-flourishing-its-in-the-numbers
Achor, Shawn. *The Happiness Advantage: How a Positive Brain Fuels Success in Work and Life.* Penguin Random House. Sept. 14, 2010.

Emmons, Robert A. *Gratitude Works!: A 21-Day Program for Creating Emotional Prosperity.* Jossey-Bass. April 1, 2013.

CHAPTER 5: ADVANCED MINDSET SKILLS

Dove Inner Critic Commercial.
https://www.youtube.com/watch?v=MOLike-Hkpg
Burns, David D. *Feeling Good: The New Mood Therapy.* Harper. Dec. 30, 2008.
Chang, Laura K. "How to Discover Automatic Thoughts." Mindfulness Muse.
https://www.mindfulnessmuse.com/cognitive-behavioral-therapy/how-to-discover-automatic-thoughts
"5 Worksheets for Challenging Negative Automatic Thoughts." Positive Psychology Program. Feb 14, 2019.
https://positivepsychologyprogram.com/challenging-automatic-thoughts-positive-thoughts-worksheets/
"Uderstanding Thoughts." Psychology Tools.
https://www.psychologytools.com/archive/understanding-thoughts/
Ackerman, Courtney. "25 CBT Techniques and Worksheets for Cognitive Behavioral Therapy." Positive Psychology Program. Mar. 20, 2017.
https://positivepsychologyprogram.com/cbt-cognitive-behavioral-therapy-techniques-worksheets/
"CBT Tools and Resources." Beck Institute.
https://beckinstitute.org/get-informed/tools-and-resources/
Neff, Kristin. "The Space Between Self-Esteem and Self-Compassion." TEDx. Feb. 6, 2013.
https://www.youtube.com/watch?v=IvtZBUSplr4
Neff, Kristin. *Self-Compassion: The Proven Power of Being Kind to Yourself.* William Morrow. June 23, 2015.
"Karpman Drama Triangle."
https://en.wikipedia.org/wiki/Karpman_drama_triangle

Forrest, Lynne. "The Three Faces of Victim – An Overview of the Victim Triangle." June 26, 2008.

https://www.lynneforrest.com/articles/2008/06/the-faces-of-victim/

Graham, Linda. "The Triangle of Victim, Rescuer, Persecutor – What it is and How to Get Out." July 24, 2017.

https://lindagraham-mft.net/triangle-victim-rescuer-persecutor-get/

Emerald, David. *The Power of TED (The Empowerment Dynamic): 10*[th] *Anniversary Edition*. Polaris Publishing. March 1, 2015.

Krajeski, Jenna. "This is Water." The New Yorker. Sept 19, 2008.

https://www.newyorker.com/books/page-turner/this-is-water

CHAPTER 7: INTRODUCTION TO HEARTSET

Kensen, Keld. "Intelligence Is Overrated: What You Really Need To Succeed." Forbes. April 12, 2012.

https://www.forbes.com/sites/keldjensen/2012/04/12/intelligence-is-overrated-what-you-really-need-to-succeed/#5e45fdb9b6d2

Capretta, Cara. Clark, Laurence P. Dai, Guangrong. "Executive Derailment: Three Cases in Point and How to Prevent It." Wiley Periodicals. Global Business and Organizational Excellence. March/April 2008.

http://www.andyhuston.com/class/BA%207040/BA%207040%20.%20Readings%20.%20Capretta.pdf

Goleman, Daniel. Boyatzis, Richard E. *Primal Leadership: Unleashing the Power of Emotional Intelligence*. Harvard Business Review Press. Aug 6, 2013.

Pease, Allan and Barbara. "The Definitive Book of Body Language."

https://www.nytimes.com/2006/09/24/books/chapters/0924-1st-peas.html

Edmondson, Amy C. "How to Turn a Group of Strangers Into a Team." TED. Feb. 9, 2019

https://www.ted.com/talks/amy_edmondson_how_to_turn_a_group_of_strangers_into_a_team/

Edmondson, Amy C. "Building a Psychologically Safe Workplace." TEDx. May 4, 2014.

https://www.youtube.com/watch?v=LhoLuui9gX8

Edmondson, Amy C. *The Fearless Organization: Creating Psychological Safety in the Workplace for Learning, Innovation, and Growth.* Wiley. Nov. 13, 2018

Porath, Christine. Pearson, Christine. "The Price of Incivility." Harvard Business Review. Jan-Feb 2013 issue.

https://hbr.org/2013/01/the-price-of-incivility

Altman, Louise. "How Emotions Shape Decision Making." The Intentional Workplace. Mar. 15, 2012.

https://intentionalworkplace.com/2012/03/15/how-emotion-shapes-decision-making/

Damasio, Antonio. *Descartes' Error: Emotion, Reason, and the Human Brain.* Putnam Publishing. Sept. 27, 2005.

Damasio, Antonio. "The Quest to Understand Consciousness." TED. Mar., 2011.

https://www.ted.com/talks/antonio_damasio_the_quest_to_understand_consciousness

Goldhill, Olivia. "Humans are Born Irrational, and That Has Made Us Better Decision-makers." Quartz. Mar. 4, 2017.

https://qz.com/922924/humans-werent-designed-to-be-rational-and-we-are-better-thinkers-for-it/

Gladwell, Malcolm. *Blink: The Power of Thinking Without Thinking.* Little, Brown and Company. Jan. 11, 2005.

Kahneman, Daniel. *Thinking, Fast and Slow.* Macmillan Publishers. April 2, 3013.

Murthy, Vivek. "Work and the Loneliness Epidemic." Harvard Business Review. Sept. 26, 2017.

https://hbr.org/cover-story/2017/09/work-and-the-loneliness-epidemic

Schawbel, Dan. "Vivek Murthy: How To Solve The Work Loneliness Epidemic." Forbes. Oct 7, 2017.

https://www.forbes.com/sites/danschawbel/2017/10/07/vivek-
    murthy-how-to-solve-the-work-loneliness-epidemic-at-work/
    #1d1dd1617172
Riordan, Christine M. "We All Need Friends at Work." Harvard Business
    Review. July 3, 2013.
https://hbr.org/2013/07/we-all-need-friends-at-work
Amortegui, Jessica. "Why Finding Meaning At Work Is More Important
    Than Feeling Happy." Fast Company. June 26, 2014.
https://www.fastcompany.com/3032126/how-to-find-meaning-
    during-your-pursuit-of-happiness-at-work
Schawbel, Dan. "Brene Brown: Why Human Connection Will Bring Us
    Closer Together." Forbes. Sept. 12, 2017.
https://www.forbes.com/sites/danschawbel/2017/09/12/brene-
    brown-why-human-connection-will-bring-us-closer-together/
    #2e63c7402f06
Pink, Daniel H. "The Puzzle of Motivation." TED. Aug. 23, 2009.
https://www.ted.com/talks/dan_pink_on_motivation
Pink, Daniel H. *Drive: The Surprising Truth About What Motivates Us.*
    Riverhead Books. April 5, 2011.

Chapter 8: Inner Heartset Skills

Taylor, Jill Bolte. *My Stroke of Insight: A Brain Scientist's Personal Journey.*
    Viking. May 12, 2008.

Chapter 9: Relational Heartset Skills

"Splitting."
https://en.wikipedia.org/wiki/Splitting_(psychology)
Bregman, Peter. "If You Want People to Listen, Stop Talking." Harvard
    Business Review. May 25, 2015.
https://hbr.org/2015/05/if-you-want-people-to-listen-stop-talking

CHAPTER 12: APPLYING YOUR MINDSET AND HEARTSET SKILLS IN THE REAL WORLD

Ruiz, Don Miguel. *The Four Agreements: A Practical Guide to Personal Freedom (A Toltec Wisdom Book)*. Amber-Allen Publishing. July 12, 2009.

Porter, Jennifer. "How to Give Feedback People Can Actually Use." Harvard Business Review. Oct. 27, 2017.

https://hbr.org/2017/10/how-to-give-feedback-people-can-actually-use

Gallo, Amy. "Giving a High Performer Productive Feedback." Harvard Business Review. Dec. 3, 2009.

https://hbr.org/2009/12/giving-a-high-performer-produc

Halford, Scott. "5 Steps for Giving Productive Feedback." Entrepreneur Magazine.

https://www.entrepreneur.com/article/219437

About the Author

DANIEL KIMBLE IS THE CEO and founder of Resonance Executive Coaching. He hosts the Unshakeable Influence podcast, and is a keynote speaker on leadership, teamwork, and culture. Daniel coaches senior executives, consults on organizational culture, and leads executive retreats and workshops for select clients.

Daniel's calling in life is his work as an executive coach and CEO. Nothing makes him happier than doing the work he was designed to do. Daniel has an adventurous and compassionate spirit, and he brings warm confidence and a sense of calm to all his endeavors. He likes to sing and play guitar, coach drivers on the racetrack, hike, mountain bike, and spend time with his family.

Daniel holds executive MBA degrees from UC Berkeley and Columbia University, an executive coaching certificate from UC Berkeley, and an undergraduate degree in computer science from UC Santa Cruz. He lives with his wife, Marianne, and son, Indiana, in the San Francisco Bay Area.

For more detailed information on Daniel, including a very fun infographic biography, please visit: ResonanceExecutiveCoaching.com.

If you have any questions or comments for Daniel, please feel free to email him at daniel@ResonanceExecutiveCoaching.com.